Stifled Laughter

One Woman's Fight
Against Censorship

Claudia Johnson

Fulcrum Publishing
Golden, Colorado

For Ormond,
who didn't want to go through it but did,
and for
Anne and Ross,
our bright future,
who will never take books for granted.

Library of Congress Cataloging-in-Publication Data

ISBN 1-55591-200-1

Printed in the United States of America
0 9 8 7 6 5 4 3 2 1

Fulcrum Publishing
350 Indiana Street, Suite 350
Golden, Colorado 80401-5093
800/992-2908

They're banning books in my backyard.
It was always an issue out thar, in
someone else's small town. Now it's here.

—Journal entry, March 10, 1986

Someday we shall recall these trials with pleasure.

—Virgil, *The Aeneid*

Prologue.

There are those who have said—and still say—that reading Chaucer will harm high school students. To date, no teens have come forward to testify that Chaucer has harmed them, but I do have intimate knowledge of one whose life was changed for the better. Allow me to witness for Chaucer:

It was 1965, a hot summer day in south Texas. My mother was finishing her master's degree, and my father was flying Hueys in some place called Saigon. I was lazing around on the living room floor, fourteen years old and bored, *bored out of my gourd*, as we used to say. I gazed up at the bookcase, plucked *The Canterbury Tales* from the shelf, and glanced at the blurb on the back. "Terrific," I said, "A bunch of pilgrims going to church."

My mother lowered the book she was reading and suggested that I read "The Miller's Tale."

I flipped the pages with utter indifference and started to read:

> Some time ago there was a rich codger
> Who lived in Oxford and took a lodger ...

As the bawdy tale began to unfold I was lurching with laughter, amazed that *literature* could be so alive, so damn funny. I had discovered what I would learn once again twenty-one years later in Lake City, Florida: literature can leap centuries and change people's lives. My vocation had declared itself, to borrow a phrase from *Lord Jim*, or, to use an expression much closer to home, I was born again.

Preface.

An increasing number of people are wringing their hands because decency is on the decline. Hell-bent to fix it, they're forming posses and galloping through our public schools to string up great writers. Books, they say, are to blame.

Most of the time they ride in from the right—the Religious *Reich*, as I've come to call it—but sometimes from the left, with political correctness and pro-censorship feminist agendas to suppress sexual material they believe degrades women. This has produced one of censorship's many rich ironies: both sides might well agree that "The Miller's Tale" should be banned.

In Lake City, Florida, where I had by first brush with the censors, the high school principal shoved "The Miller's Tale" under my nose and snarled in my face, "Ain't you think that's *po*nography?" I pointed out that Chaucer was funny and *po*nography usually wasn't. The principal scowled, and I realized in a slow-burn gag kind of way that censors find funny offensive.

"This material makes crass humor out of a potentially serious problem in our society," droned the preacher who demanded that Chaucer be banned. "The problem being of sex as a plaything between adults or adolescents with little or no commitment and no regard for consequences."

Those of us who joined forces for Chaucer tried pointing out that there *were* consequences. "The basic moral of 'The Miller's Tale,'" one Chaucerian wrote, "is that anybody who fools around with adultery and promiscuity is going to get his ass burned in this life and the next." The censors did not crack a smile.

This was eight years ago. I had a hunch it was just the beginning.

It was. Censorship has increased beyond my wildest nightmares. It is now so pervasive there's an article about it each week in the paper. Sometimes two. Recently it was the banning of Alice Walker's story "Am I Blue?" from a California state-wide English text because it was "anti-meat," and an excerpt from Annie Dillard's *An American Childhood* because its depiction of a snowball fight was too violent.

In case you're laughing—and I hope you are—let me assure you the censors are not. Whatever their political stripes, those who ban books have one thing in common—a deadly seriousness. They ain't got no sense of humor.

Consider the school that banned *The Stupids Step Out* (my daughter's favorite book as a child) because "it teaches kids to flunk classes" (my daughter is currently tied for valedictorian of her high school class) and its sequel *The Stupids Have a Ball* because the illustration of Mrs. Stupid wearing a chicken on her head "promotes cruelty to animals."

When Chaucer is ponography and snowball fights are too violent and the Stupids can't step out anymore, it isn't decency that's in danger, it's our sense of humor. At the rate we're going, we'll join the Top Ten Historic Humorless Hits—the Spanish Inquisition, Nazi Germany, McCarthy's America—(sing along if you know the words), and in case you doubt this is true, check out the book banning statistics during those times. Now there's something to wring hands about.

The antidote, as Chaucer well knew, is laughter itself. Sean O'Casey called it "wine for the soul … brought in to mock at things as they are so that they may topple down, and make room for better things to come."

I wrote this book because I believe there are better thing to come for this country than grim-faced censors banning great books in the name of decency and moral correctness. The trouble is, we won't know what these better things are unless we laugh, howl, guffaw at the madness around us: *Red Riding Hood* promotes alcoholism. *Snow White* promotes violence. *Of Mice and Men* teaches students to talk like migrant workers. *In the Night Kitchen* promotes nudity.

I could go on.

I wrote this book to help people laugh, not because I think censorship isn't a serious matter, but because I know that it is. As William Zinsser put it, "I want to make people laugh so that they'll see things seriously." Lucky for us, a major element of comedy is "rigid reverence" and "inelasticity," as Henri Bergson wrote in his essay on laughter. This may be the richest irony of all: The more self-righteous and rigid the censors become, the more they become laughingstock.

Not that I didn't lose my own sense of humor during these fights. I did, again and again. I might have lost it for good if it weren't for those people who helped to restore it. I cannot thank them enough.

In Lake City, my co-plaintiffs, Susan Davis and Jim and Monya Virgil, were fearless and funny. We spent hundreds of hours together in each other's kitchens, on the phone, at school board meetings, and in federal court. My friends Jan, Sharon, Dennis, David, Grant, Ben, Stowe, Meredith, Forrest, and Noah—also went to meetings, wrote letter, called the censors *bozos* in public, took care of my children (and me) and taught me how to play Liverpool.

In Live Oak, the English faculty at the high school and the librarians were profiles in courage. Sherry Millington came to my defense when I needed it most. And we all needed Barbara Ceryak's humor, open mind, and advice.

Leanne Katz and her staff at the National Coalition Against Censorship provided ongoing perspective, support, and information, as did the A.C.L.U. I am especially grateful to Sam Jacobson for taking our case and defending the First Amendment so eloquently.

During both fights, I had the strange (and slightly schizophrenic) experience of living in towns where literature was reviled, and commuting to Florida State University where it was revered. Twice a week I returned to the book-banning fray with my sense of humor and purpose renewed. John Fenstermaker provided hilarious Victorian synonyms for Lake City (Dismal Seepage, Boggleywollah). Jerry Stern taught me the shapes of fiction and kept me laughing throughout ("put a little English on that sentence") and Janet Burroway—the most generous person I know—put me up, fed me, and showed me what a friend and writer could be. I am grateful, too, for her P.E.N./*Newman's Own* First Amendment Award Nomination. Robyn Allers, Pam Ball, and Barbara Hamby also continue to show me why good friends and writing matter so much.

Peter Stowell introduced me to film and hired me at the Film School. My colleagues and students and the aptly-named support staff there have been a great help as I've finished this book. Meryl Warren guided me through many levels of technical morass. Charlie Boyd, Steve Chase, and some of my screenwriting students helped me brainstorm subtitles. Charlie found the final quote for the book, and I am typing this preface on a computer he loaned me. And I dough there's a faculty or staff anywhere that laughs more than we do.

During the shooting of *Schindler's List*, Steven Spielberg called Robin Williams for comic relief; during the fights in Lake City and Live Oak, I called my lanky friend, Stuart Hample, who also introduced me to Mildred Marmur, my dedicated agent. I thank her and also Bob Baron, Tammy Ferris, Linda Stark, and Sandy Trupp at Fulcrum for loving the book.

On the homefront, my mother came up with Stifled Laughter and rescued me from what Jerry Stern calls Title Hell. But the debt goes much deeper than that. All during my happy childhood, she gave us time to talk and laugh at the table. Humor was truth, truth, humor. If you had a funny story to tell, others would shut up and listen. Her own outspoken style taught me what irrepressible meant. And I wouldn't be telling this story at all if she hadn't introduced me to Chaucer when I was fourteen.

My father and sister are natural wags and wonderful laughers. This has helped me more than they know. So have my father's scotch mists; in fact, this story began over one of his masterpieces, which he has cheerfully administered since.

But my greatest thanks—and admiration—goes to my husband and children who had to live with me during these embattled, emotional years. My outbursts were (and are) constantly tempered by my husband's dry humor. And our children—who have grown up reading banned books—are living proof that the censors are wrong.

Finally, thanks to the late Geoffrey Chaucer. I owe to him my education in English; The least I could do is defend his place in our English education.

March 29, 1994

A Note on Methodology.

From the beginning, the fight to restore literary classics to the classroom seemed important, historic. With the help of Susan Davis and Monya Virgil, I kept careful records as the story unfolded. The school board meetings are transcribed from tape recording made by the school boards themselves. Courtroom scenes are taken from transcriptions of court proceedings made by the court reporter. Phone conversations are taken from transcriptions I made as the conversations occurred, Excerpts from newspapers and magazines are taken verbatim from the publications, and journal entries or excerpts are taken from the journal that I kept at the time.

One.

March 8, 1986.

I'm sitting by my father's pool in south Florida. It's a pleasant spring night; the mullet are jumping in the deep water canal beyond the pool's screened enclosure. My husband, the folklorist Ormond Loomis, is regaling my father about life in Lake City, the small north Florida town where we live. Anne and Ross, our two children, are already sleeping.

I lean back, close my eyes, let the ice from my scotch mist melt on my tongue. I've just passed my doctoral exams in English at Florida State, six months of nothing but study, stacks of books and three-by-five cards, soup to nuts, the Greeks to the present. I'm tired.

Ormond mentions a minister back in Lake City, a man named Fritz Fountain, who wants the school board to ban the high school humanities textbook because two selections— *Lysistrata* and "The Miller's Tale"—promote, in the preacher's opinion, women's lib and pornography.

I set down my scotch mist and snap, "He did *what*?"

It's one of those moments that keeps me guessing about a Great Design. After reading more than two hundred plays, I decided that *Lysistrata* is the finest stage comedy written, a rare breed of play where women are victors not victims, and "The Miller's Tale," as Ormond well knows, is the reason I'm studying English at all. (He's heard the story so often he likes to joke that he could motif it.)

I can tell by the look on his face—those brown eyes getting bigger—that he knows what I'm thinking.

"Oh, don't get involved," he says, "please don't get involved. They'll be burning crosses on our front yard."

Lake City lies at the heart of Columbia County in the Suwannee Valley region of rural north Florida. The county stretches fifty-odd miles from Georgia to the Santa Fe River, but the iced-tea-colored water of the more famous Suwannee forms the county's northwestern border and gives the region its name.

A small conservative town—population roughly ten thousand—Lake City is built among live oaks and a half-dozen lakes fished by long-necked long-legged birds—heron, anhinga, and cormorant—who are hunted in turn by a prolific population of gators. More than once as I jogged around Lake Desoto, I've stepped into the street to avoid an alligator sunning itself on the cypress-mulch path.

Alligator was once the town's name, as the historical marker in the town square will tell you:

> Originally called Alpata Telophka, or Alligator Town, this site was a Seminole village ruled by the powerful chief Alligator, an instigator of the Dade Massacre, which began the great Seminole War in 1835. Following the cessation of hostilities, a white settlement sprang up on the site of the old Seminole village and became known simply as Alligator. Prior to the War Between the States, the name was changed to Lake City.

One wag in the state legislature suggested changing it to Crocodile, but proponents of Lake City prevailed.

Not far from the historical marker, a white marble obelisk commemorates the 151 Confederate soldiers who lost their lives at the Battle of Olustee fifteen miles east of Lake City on February 20, 1864. Each February, in what is now the Olustee National Forest, the battle is reenacted, a two day event preceded by a parade down Marion Street, school bands and twirlers and cartwheeling gymnasts sharing the spotlight with women in hoop skirts and men in once-a-year-beards who stop now and then and fire their muskets at the slate-colored sky.

Settled by people from Georgia and South Carolina, Lake City is culturally more akin to these states than to mid or south Florida. Cultural experts—my husband among them—have wryly observed that the farther north you travel in Florida, the more South you get. This is gradually changing as the town sprawls west toward I-75. The downtown, graced by the square and the old Blanche Hotel, is dying. Most shops have moved out to the mall; a few diehards haven't, though they probably will as the population expands. State and national demographics are changing. Tired of traffic and crime and crowds and cement, not to mention Hurricane Andrew, many south Floridians are now moving north. The hospitable climate and taxes in Florida are bringing more northerners south. And a large cult, the End-Timers, selected Lake City as its new home, causing no small consternation among the Old Guard.

Not that they haven't created troubles of their own. Over the years, persistent corruption among the Old Guard has given Lake City—located near the intersection of Interstates 10 and 75—the nickname "the crossroads of corruption," or, as I prefer saying, "where Christ meets corruption."

While Chaucer and Aristophanes were being condemned as immoral, Lake City's Police Chief Ray Simmons was admitting to a litany of thefts during his six years as chief," according to the April 14, 1986 *Lake city Reporter.* "Among the charges: stealing guns and money from the department's evidence room and pocketing more than $1,015 he helped raise for St. Jude's Children's Hospital." He was convicted and sentenced to five years probation.

A year earlier, former Columbia County Sheriff Steve Spradley had been sentenced to ten years in prison for three federal counts of mail fraud, filing a false income tax return and permitting a felon to possess a firearm. This was the result of a plea bargain with prosecutors who dropped racketeering and drug charges, touchy subjects in town since the 1977 sentencing of Circuit Judge Samuel S, Smith to three years in federal prison for possessing and conspiring to distribute 1,600 pounds of marijuana.

When Smith was indicted, Mayor Gerald Witt remarked, "There's enough corruption in Columbia County to keep the preachers preaching and the lawyers lying for a long time to come." Nine years later, when Ray Simmons was convicted, Witt told the *Florida Times Union* that he filet the days of the "old buddy system" had finally come to an end.

An editorial in the *Lake City Reporter* hoped Witt was right:

> For much too long, the names of Lake City and Columbia County have been synonymous with crime and corruption, with greed and lust, with narcotics and easy money and prostitution and a sleazy lifestyle built on depravity and man's desire to serve the worst in himself.

The editorial appeared on May 22, 1986, five days before the Superintendent dismissed "The Miller's Tale" and *Lysistrata* as "super crude" and one board member stood by his decision to ban them because, as he said, "we have morals to stand up to."

There's a frontier feeling in town, an uneasy meeting of Old Guard and New marked by a distrust of outsiders that Bundy made worse when he kidnapped and murdered the Lake City junior high student, Kimberly Leach. References to "real Columbian Countians" are still made at city council or county commission meetings in town. Bob Murray, host of the local radio talk show, "Speak Out," remarked one night that after ten years he still had not been granted his "citizenship."

Some of the distrust may be deserved: Outsiders are not always kind to Lake City. A British visitor in 1854, Charles Lanman, wrote in his book *Adventures in the Wilds of the United States and British American Provinces*, "The opinion that I formed of the people generally who lived secluded in these piney woods, was that they were uniformly kind and obliging, moral as could be expected, but certainly not over-burdened with intelligence." Fifty years later, however, the town was considered "a center of learning" when the legislature named Lake City's Florida Agriculture College the "University of Florida," but after two years the state board of education voted to move the institution to Gainesville. Angry mobs in Lake City couldn't change the board's mind, and the town lost its claim to educational excellence. The Kindergarten Center may win awards every year, and the enrollment may be growing at Lake City Community College (founded in 1962), but this goes against a strong anti-intellectual current in town. The phrase "pointy-headed intellectual" still appears now and then in a letter to the editor of the *Lake City Reporter*, Don Caldwell, who advised me, when this book embranglement started, to keep my Ph.D. work a secret—there were those who would hold it against me. Amazingly, no textbook had ever been openly challenged until March 1986. The complaint took the town by surprise, not because someone thought the two classics were dirty, but because someone had read them at all. As one wit in city government put it, "Everyone knows, if you want to hide anything in Lake City, you put it in a book."

That a preacher objected surprised no one at all. Lake City is dominated by churches, eighty-two at last count. Signs for churches crowd the roadsides at Burma Shave intervals. Signs in front of churches offer sight-bites of sermons:

> FEAR IS THE DARKROOM
> WHERE SATAN TAKES YOU
> TO DEVELOP YOUR NEGATIVES

The leading denomination is, of course, Southern Baptist, represented west of I-75 by the Berea Baptist Church whose pastor, Fritz Fountain, had asked the school board to ban the humanities textbook. His reasons were outlined more fully in the March 6 *Lake City Reporter* that lay in our yard when we got home from my father's:

> Fountain, pastor of Berea Baptist Church, said excerpts from the play *Lysistrata* by Aristophanes were "offensive" because they were sexually explicit.
>
> Fountain said he also found several study questions at the end of the play offensive.
>
> One question asked, "Is the sexual explicitness in *Lysistrata* comic? Compare the treatment of sex here with the deadly seriousness of pornography.

What is the difference?"

Another literary piece in the textbook, "The Miller's Tale," also contained offensive passages, noted Fountain.

In his complaint to Superintendent Silas Pittman and members of the school board, Fountain said the "offensive language" he pointed out hampered society in its efforts to combat teenage sexual promiscuity.

"This material makes crass humor out of a potentially serious problem in our society," Fountain wrote in his complaint. "The problem being of sex as a plaything between immature adults or adolescents with little or no commitment and no regard for consequences."

I held up the headline—MINISTER WANTS CHS HUMANITIES BOOK BANNED. Ormond rolled his eyes heavenward and ushered Ross, four, and Anne, eight, into the house.

I followed him, raving. "How can *Lysistrata* be sexually explicit? Wives *withhold* sex. Absence of sex is the *point*. And "The Miller's Tale" makes fun of our society's problems? It was written in the late 1300s! I can just see the headline"—I waved my hand through the air—"CHAUCER AND ARISTOPHANES BUSTED ON SIX COUNTS OF PORN."

Ormond laughed, but later, getting ready for bed, he reminded me that I had a dissertation to write and two children who needed their mother. He didn't mention himself, how little time we'd had for each other since I'd gone back to school. "Look," he said, "I just hope you won't get involved."

"I hope I won't have to."

Looking back, I understand that he wasn't worried about burning crosses, he was worried about another marathon. We'd just finished one: for two years I'd been commuting four hundred miles a week to finish my coursework at Florida State. I'd spent every Monday and Wednesday night in Tallahassee; he'd taken care of the house and the kids and his job and he'd handled it well, real grace under pressure, but he was worn down and he had this terrible feeling that a censorship fight could go on for years.

On Monday morning, March 10, I took his advice and returned to my dissertation, a comic novel about a playwright, Roz Lawson, who wants to get out of Ohumpka, a small repressive north Florida town—fiction, har har de har. I'd written the first two chapters for Jerry Stern's novel workshop; when her husband says he'll leave Ohumpka if she beats his salary, Roz takes a job on a new soap, *Heart's Curtain.*

The idea had risen like swamp gas from two episodes in my life—the six long years in Lake City and an eight-month stint as a dialogist on the world's worst soap opera, *The Catlins.*

Like my heroine Roz, I'd followed my folklorist husband to rural north Florida. An academic *naif,* I assumed all the world was a campus—stimulating, book-loving, enlightened. Ormond and I had met doing graduate work in folklore at Indiana University in Bloomington, a wonderful town. We married, had our first baby, and bought our first house, a one-room cabin overlooking Lake Lemon. I finished my M.A. in folklore and worked full-time on campus while Ormond finished his Ph.D. During lunch I took playwriting classes in the theatre department, and I fell in love with this collaborative art.

After co-founding a children's theatre group, Six Bit Players, I began writing plays. My work was produced at I.U., in the American College Theatre Festival, and in the Festival of New American Plays at Actors Theatre of Louisville, where one reviewer said I offered "hope for humanity." Mel Gussow said I was "wrily amusing."

In 1980, when Ormond finished his Ph.D., he was offered a job at the Bureau of Florida Folklife in White Springs, a town on the Suwannee of roughly 700 people. There were no homes for sale in White Springs, so we bought one in nearby Lake City—a two-story house built in 1907 that backed on a Civil War era Episcopal Church.

At the time, the move made good sense. My career was on track; writing, after all, was a portable profession. Ormond would work on the annual Florida Folk Festival; I would work on my plays. And it would be a homecoming of sorts—he grew up in Clearwater and I was born in Ft. Lauderdale.

The first thing I thought of when we drove into Lake City

was a line from Denise Levertov, something about small towns she might have died in. There were days that I thought I was dying. The first question everyone asked was, "What's your home church?" A neighbor's overweight husband got down on his knees in my kitchen and witnessed for Christ. The carpenter who built the shelves in my study witnessed, too—he said he was fluent in Old and New Tongues. If I mentioned my work as a playwright, people nodded politely and recommended Jesus. Everywhere that I looked people were walking with Jesus, talking with Jesus, taking their troubles to Jesus—our baby-sitter called it "kneeology." They talked about "wearing Jesus" and that's what they did, on hats, T-shirts, bumper stickers—JESUS IS LORD IN COLUMBIA COUNTY—IN CASE OF RAPTURE THIS CAR WILL BE UNMANNED. I felt suffocated, the big soft pillow of Jesus pressed down on my face.

Ormond and I joined the First Presbyterian Church that overlooks Lake Montgomery in the heart of Lake City. I edited the church newsletter, *Presby Press*, for a year. Our pastor, Ed Montgomery, commissioned a short play for the church's 125th anniversary, and the play was a hit, but I felt lost, God, I felt lost, a feeling that lasted for years, summed up in a 1984 journal entry when Ross was three: "With Ross in Publix, turned up the wrong aisle and said out loud, 'Where am I?' Ross pointed at me and said, 'You're right there.'"

Other journal entries alternate between cries of frustration and self-recrimination because I wasn't "sitting full in the moment," as Least-Heat Moon said in *Blue Highways*, because I was not more engaged in what he calls "the god-awful difficulty of just paying attention":

> Poured all of this out to my mother—this desolate little town—the lack of opportunity for me—but the recurring kindnesses—Buddy saying Anne was a "lovely lady,"—Ed's sermon on Sunday recounting the story of the olive wood box—how people could leave a scroll of their troubles on the altar but on one condition: they had to take away the troubles of another and no one did.
>
> How ashamed I feel to complain but there are

times I think I'm dying, at least the ambition.

I wrote plays as long as I could without theatres, directors, or actors in town. I arranged childcare two days a week and I finished my third full-length play *Y*, but the writing got harder and harder, and I began to understand what Tennessee Williams meant when he said a writer's first concern must be "to discover that magic place of all places where the work goes better than it has gone before, the way that a gasoline motor picks up when you switch it from regular to high octane. For one of the mysterious things about writing is the extreme susceptibility it shows to the influence of places."

Lake City was far from magic for me. I enjoyed—and still do—the natural beauty of rural north Florida and the state's rich folk culture, but I felt disconnected, marooned, a secular humorist in a God-fearing town. I understood why Romeo cries, "Say not banishment!" Why Chekhov's three sisters keep up their mournful chorus of exile, "Oh, Moscow, Moscow, Moscow."

As antidote, I read Marjorie Rawlings—hadn't she thrived in Cross Creek?—but she wasn't a playwright. I was, and a playwright, I was learning, cannot flourish alone. By 1982, my career felt like the end of Molier's *Misanthrope*, a *diminuendo*, a dying fall. I was considering a career in landscape architecture when my former playwriting teacher, Sam Smiley, called one day in December. He'd taken a sabbatical from Indiana to be the headwriter for a new soap that was based in Atlanta. He offered me a job writing dialogue.

"C'mon, Sam," I laughed.

"I'm not kidding. I think you'd be good."

A wryly amusing writer, writing soap? Writing what Thurber once called "unrelieved murk." I'd only seen one soap in my life, when Anne had the chicken pox. The more I watched the more I marveled—*nothing happened*. The chief narrative device, it seemed to me, was retardation. It was more interesting watching Anne scratch her pox.

What was left of my artistic self cried out against it, nay, belly-laughed, but was finally drowned out by what Williams calls "the desperate necessity for the companionship of one's own kind."

I took the job.

I enjoyed working with Sam and getting away to Atlanta, but I learned a valuable lesson which Roz also learns in the novel: a comic writer cannot find happiness writing for a humorless medium any more than she can find happiness living in a humorless town. For eight months, I put my playwriting aside and mastered the essential tag of all soap opera scenes—the long take on someone's anguished face. (If anyone smiles, it's just a signal more trouble is coming.) There were weeks I wrote four gloomy episodes of *The Catlins*. I began living more in their living room than my own. I saw my family at mealtime, but all they got from me was a long anguished look. By the end of March I was crying into my scrambled eggs. Ormond suggested that I get some help.

I went to see Pat Korb, a Gestalt therapist down in Gainesville. Pat looks a little like Gertrude Stein—short, straight gray cap-cut hair, a warm laugh and a big box of Kleenex. I told her a recurring nightmare I was having: I am sitting at a campfire surrounded by darkness. A person appears on the edge of the light, leaping and screaming for my attention. She is neglected, starving. I know if I don't pay attention to her, she will die.

The person, I realized, was my sense of humor.

Not that *The Catlins* wasn't a riot sometimes—it just didn't *mean* to be funny. It was so bad, so low budget, there were no experienced actors or second takes. The actor who played the soap's patriarch, T. J. Catlin, was a Southeast Conference referee. There were episodes when a phone didn't ring but he answered it anyway. Other times, he got tangled up in the wires. The producer's mother, Babs, was one of the writers.

Across America, people began to tune in for laughs. A Cleveland columnist wondered if it was a deliberate spoof. John Carman, television critic for the *Atlanta Constitution*, called it "a comedy about incompetent Atlantans who stumble over each other in a cardboard box of a mansion." Lewis Grizzard pleaded for killing the show "before it spread across the nation like an outbreak of mouth sores."

It was mercifully canceled after two years. I was fired after eight months, in August 1983, not that anyone bothered to tell me (Sam had been fired a few months before). I got the news from a clipping my father sent from the *Miami Herald*, an article about *The Catlins'* new team of writers. I read it, amazed, then I punched in the studio's calling card number to find out if I still had a job. The operator informed me the number was no longer valid.

I decided it was time to go back to school.

A year later at Florida State, during the fall of 1984, I wrote an essay about my soap misadventures for Jerry Stern's pop culture class. Jerry thought the essay was an excellent outline for a novel—so I, once a playwright, decided to write one for my dissertation.

On March 10, 1986, I was working on chapter three when the telephone rang. It was a friend, Susan Davis, a firebrand with a Port St. Joe drawl. She wanted to know if I'd seen Fritz Fountain's complaint in the paper. I told her I had.

"Well, *what*," she said, "are we going to do?"

She'd been wielding that question since she moved to Lake City in 1983 so her husband, Doug, could direct the Chamber of Commerce. She'd just aimed it at our children's gifted program, and we'd spent several months organizing Parents for the Enhancement of the Enrichment Program, fondly referred to as P.E.E.P. One of the parents we'd worked with was school board member Dianne Lane, a close friend of Susan's. I asked what Lane had to say about Reverend Fountain's complaint.

"Oh, she thinks he's got a good point," Susan said, "*Lysistrata* takes the Lord's name in vain."

I blinked. "But it was written in 411 B.C. The Lord was *Zeus*." *Toto, I don't think we're in Kansas anymore.*

"It may sound crazy," she said, "but a whole lot of people agree."

Later that day I wrote in my journal:

> By the time Susan and I finished talking, I felt as though I'd had two quarts of coffee. My hands were shaking. There was no hope for continuing work on my novel, I knew, and a phrase from Grace Paley rose up from the landfill of my mind, some-

thing her character Faith said about *wanting* to return library books but not doing it: "I *had* promised my children to end the war before they grew up." Somehow the thought of books being banned seemed more important than how I rendered Roz's first soap story conference in chapter three.

I told Susan I'd call Silas Pittman, the superintendent, and find out what I could. After all, he attended the Episcopal church, and we had a nodding acquaintance across my back fence.

One of the good things about life in a small town like Lake City is the accessibility of public officials. The school board secretary didn't ask who I was or why I was calling; she put my call through. Pittman was pleasant, a born politician, until I told him I'd just heard about Fountain's complaint and asked what had brought it about. There was a long loaded silence. He asked how much I wanted to know. I said the whole story.

Pittman said that Fountain's daughter, Leigh Ann, had taken the humanities class, an elective, the previous fall. *Lysistrata* was not required, but one day the teacher—Norman Choice, the high school chorus director—finished his lesson before the hour was up. He told the class to turn to the next selection and, for the remaining moments, they read *Lysistrata* aloud.

After school, Leigh Ann Fountain told her father about it. She also showed him "The Miller's Tale" which she'd found on her own. Fountain was deeply offended by the words "piss" and "ass" in "The Miller's Tale" and "god damn" in *Lysistrata*.

Pittman said he had to agree. "I might could live with 'arse,' he said, "but 'ass' is too much. Both works should be read in the original."

There was a pause.

"But Dr. Pittman," I said, "they're in Greek and Middle English."

"Well, then," he said, "a different translation."

What bothered Reverend Fountain the most was "the E.R.A. stuff, the feminist angle," and Pittman said it bothered him, too.

I suggested that a different translation would not change

the play's outcome, then I thanked him for his time. "I wanted to hear it directly from you so I wouldn't overreact."

"Oh, I'm not sure it would be an overreaction," he said. "There's no telling how far Reverend Fountain will go."

Troubled by this last remark, I called Ed Montgomery at the Presbyterian Church. A well-educated, articulate man with deep roots in Columbia County (his father had been pastor of the same church from 1926 to 1966), he would know what to do.

Ed said he knew Fountain; they had gone head to head a few years before over licensing liquor. "He's a smart man," he said, "but you can be smart and ... "

There was a pause. I finished his thought. "Ignorant?"

"Yes."

As small town life would have it, Leigh Ann Fountain took piano lessons from Ed's wife, June. He told me she'd arrived at her last lesson extremely upset. The March 7 *Lake City Reporter* had run a nasty tongue-in-cheek editorial supporting her father's request that the board ban the humanities textbook:

> The good reverend is not only right, but has barely scratched the surface of the problem. Banning those two works is but a mere start; indeed, what is needed here is a total ban on reading in the school system. A child who does not and cannot read cannot be influenced by what he reads. A high-schooler cannot read the word "sex" and have 15 years of moral training come unraveled. Knowing how to read and then turning that ability into a license to broaden one's own horizons can only lead to one evil and despicable thing: Learning!"

June Montgomery told Leigh Ann that it's one thing to have private feelings about a book but all that changes when it becomes public, and she really should have thought about that before she began making accusations. The girl said she was sorry but she couldn't back down. Ed thought Fountain was just backing his daughter. "They've been teaching Chaucer and Aristophanes in Columbia County for fifty years," he reassured me. "I don't think they'll stop teaching them now."

I wrote all this in my journal, which, looking back, seems prophetic:

> After talking to Ed, I went for a two-mile walk around Lake Desoto. I thought about *Lysistrata*, the play. How Aristophanes was a conservative, how the play is about saving the country, keeping the family together, values Fritz Fountain is probably for. It's not about sex, it's about passive resistance and peace. But the fact is, the women win.
>
> By the time I got home I was laughing to myself. I'd worked out a treatment for a screenplay about a small town where women discover *Lysistrata* and the power they have over men. *Lysistrata, The Movie.* The play changes their marriages and their lives.

It never occurred to me that it might change mine.

Two.

The textbook in question—Volume I of *The Humanities, Cultural Roots and Continuities*, published by Heath—had passed the state evaluation procedure in 1980 and was the only entry under humanities in the Catalog of State-Adopted Instructional Materials. Educators at Columbia County High School had reviewed and adopted the book in 1981, and it had been in use ever since. No one had complained about this or any other state-approved textbook before, so Fountain's complaint caught the school board with their procedural pants down.

At their meeting on March 11, Pittman proposed an emergency procedure for the school board to vote on. If approved, it would then be adopted into the regular School Board Policy Manual at a public hearing on April 8.

Board member Roger Little, who directed the Lake City Recreation Department, moved to adopt the emergency rule as presented by Pittman. Keith Hudson, a graying salesman at McDuffy's Sporting Goods, seconded the motion. The remaining members of the board—Dianne Lane, Jack Haltiwanger, a retired voc-ed teacher, and Dickie Chappell, owner of North Florida Fence and Pool, all concurred.

The next morning Susan Davis drove to the school board building—a squat yellow brick structure up the street from our house on Hernando—and picked up a copy of Pittman's "Proposed New Policy On Challenged State Adopted Textbooks." It invited complainants like Reverend Fountain to submit their objections in writing to the superintendent who would forward the complaint to a textbook review committee.

We were pleased with the guidelines the textbook committee would have to follow:

1. Read all books or examine material referred to in the complaint.
2. Check general acceptance of the material by reading reviews and consulting authoritative lists.
3. Weigh values and faults against each other and form opinions based on the material as a whole and not only on passage pulled out of context.
5. [sic] Discuss the material and prepare a report and/or recommendation of the committee's findings.
6. File a copy of the report and/or recommendation with the Superintendent for submission to the School Board for final dispositions. Irrespective of the report or recommendation of the textbook committee, the school board may remove any material from the school which it considers inappropriate or undesirable.

"Which means," Susan said, "the textbook committee can go to a whole lot of trouble deciding these works are okay, and the school board can do whatever it pleases."

We decided to contact other north Florida superintendents and find out what procedures they followed. Union County, the smallest in Florida, asked parents to read potentially controversial books (Steinbeck was a favorite fundamentalist target) and sign a permission slip saying their child could read it. Students whose parents objected were offered an alternative text. The right of other students to receive information was not restricted. Leon County, home to the capital, Tallahassee, and Florida State, followed a similar course. I made notes and an appointment with Pittman.

Silas Pittman is a big beefy man with tight gray curls, narrow eyes, and a wide friendly smile. A popular speaker at Elks or Rotary, he earned an E.Ed. with a dissertation on transportation from Nova University back in the seventies. The morning I went to see him at his office, he'd been serving as the Columbia County superintendent, except for one term, since 1970.

He leaned back in his chair and listened as I outlined the other counties' procedures, but he flatly refused to offer alternative texts.

I said, "Surely it's better than banning these classics." He disagreed. "What if parents don't believe in evolution? Do I give their child a creationist text?"

"Dr. Pittman," I said, "couldn't you write a procedure that limited alternative selections to literature? That's what Union and Leon counties have done."

Pittman stood up. Apparently our meeting was over. He walked past me and opened the door. "If you want to discuss your idea with the board, you're welcome to come to the April 8 hearing."

The next morning, over coffee, Susan and I discussed the matter with her friend and board member, Dianne Lane, the spitting image of Lily Tomlin as the telephone operator. We told her about Union and Leon county's procedures and Pittman's objections. Dianne was reluctant to argue with Pittman; she wrung her hands at the thought.

"Dianne," I said. "Has the board *ever* voted against Pittman's wishes?"

"No, never," she sighed. She agreed to ask her fellow board members to consider an alternative textbook procedure instead of the one that Pittman had written.

Meanwhile, I called Silas Pittman and asked if I could attend the meetings of the textbook committee. He said I was welcome to do that.

On the way to their first meeting, I stopped by the school board building and picked up a list of people on the committee: David Ellis, principal of the high school; James Henry Tyre, the director of county-wide Media Services; Barbara Foreman, director of secondary education; and members of the secondary textbook committee, Jack Rankin, William Orr, Richard Romine, and Morris Williams. I picked up a copy of their credentials and braced myself for the worst: Of the seven members, only two—Barbara Foreman and Morris Williams—had any advanced education in English.

The committee met in Mr. Ellis's office out at the high school, a windowless room with his desk at one end and a seminar table and chairs at the other. The committee was already seated when I arrived. They seemed a little startled to see me—I was the only parent who'd asked to attend—but manners prevailed and they offered me a chair by the blackboard.

I sat there, set apart like a dunce, a friendly grin on my face. Since the hearing, I'd decided the best tack was to be as cheerful as possible, so when David Ellis rolled back the cover of the oversized paperback text and shoved a page from "The Miller's Tale" under my nose and growled in my ear, "Ain't you think that's pornography?" I smiled and agreed it was bawdy but pointed out it was also quite funny, and pornography usually wasn't. I showed him the study question that had offended Fritz Fountain: "Is the sexual explicitness in *Lysistrata* comic? Compare the treatment of sex here with the deadly seriousness of pornography. What is the difference?" Ellis slumped into his chair at the head of the table, a man who wanted to be somewhere else.

James Henry Tyre asked if Fountain's objection was to the whole book or just the two selections. Ellis shrugged. "If it's to the selections, there are alternatives," Tyre said. "If it's the book, there is no other humanities book approved by the state."
"We could eliminate humanities from the curriculum," Ellis said, perking up slightly.

Barbara Foreman protested. "But the course isn't required, so a person who finds it distasteful doesn't have to enroll."

Jack Rankin sat drumming his fingers. "The kids we talked to said they thought they could handle it. If my reading is any indication, just about all writing anymore could be challenged." Foreman nodded. "Some say the Holy Book is full of dirty passages."

Tyre chuckled. "You think we ought to sing that Song of Solomon to old Father Fountain?"

"David, Bathsheba," mused Rankin. "We use that text out here also. Should we cut that selection or stop teaching the text?"

There was a brief discussion about whether or not the photograph of Michaelangelo's *David* in chapter eleven was pornographic. The committee decided it wasn't, then Ellis asked those who had read the two challenged works if they were prepared to discuss them.

They weren't. Most hadn't had time to read them.

Ellis adjourned until March 27 when they would meet again and write their report. "We'll write a majority and minority opinion if we have to. If we split, the school board will choose."

On March 26 I wrote a letter to Pittman and asked to be placed on the agenda at the April 8 hearing. If he was so hotly opposed to alternative texts, and the board had never opposed him, I doubted they would listen to Lane, but before they adopted Pittman's procedure, I wanted to propose a change of my own.

Ormond came home while I was typing the letter. He frowned, concerned again that this was leading me away from writing my dissertation. He was right. I'd spent the last couple of weeks talking to superintendents and poring over procedures and combing the Dudley Fitts translation of *Lysistrata* to count dirty words (there are two). Now I was writing a letter to Pittman instead of finishing chapter three of my novel.

I explained that writing the letter wasn't easy for me. Neither was arguing with Pittman about his procedure or pressuring Lane to offer another. Standing up in front of the school board—none of whom I knew except Lane—scared the hell out of me. I'd kept a low profile in town. I wasn't used to speaking in public. I was not a crusader. A coward was more like it: Once, when my fellow students were wearing black armbands to protest Vietnam, I pinned a strip of yellow cloth down the back of my shirt. People laughed, which was the point. If I had a cause, it was comedy, and two of the greatest comic writers were under attack.

"If I don't speak up," I told Ormond, "these works could

be censored. If I don't speak up, I've censored myself."

The textbook committee reconvened on March 27, Ormond's and my eleventh anniversary.

"We're glad you're here," Barbara Foreman said when I walked in the door.

"Yes," Ellis said, "we appreciate your coming."

I smiled and took my seat by the blackboard.

Ellis began by reviewing his notes on *Lysistrata* taken, he said, from *Masterplots*: "*Lysistrata* was the most frequently produced Greek drama in the contemporary theatre. 'Make Love Not War' sums up the attitude of this play. It carries a more important theme than sexuality; sex was a mere weapon used to bring about peace. The playwright is scolding men of that time: if they couldn't put an end to war in twenty years, they might as well give up. It has a respected dramatic structure, one of few that has survived. First produced in 411 when Athens' fortune was at its lowest point. An excellent play whose theme and broad humor are readily accessible to contemporary audiences. Mingled farce, beautiful poetry and serious commentary on contemporary society. Aristophanes was regarded as the greatest poet of Old Comedy, but there's no escaping the fact that Aristophanes wrote obscenely."

Barbara Foreman said her research agreed. "The author was trying to show that women can stop war and men can't. Aristophanes is recognized as one of the greatest Greek dramatists; we are lucky to have a few of his great works. The theme is to stop war. The women are trying to save the young men who have been in the war for twenty years so women will have men they can marry. The theme is not sex at all."

"And all the definitions I've seen of obscene literature or pornography had 'no artistic value' included," Tyre added. "I don't know that this fits that definition." He glanced at his notes. "A somewhat bawdy skeptical work of art."

"Personally myself," Ellis said, "the words and expressions in the play would not be objectionable for a person of senior high level to better understand that period of Greek literature. Based on the material as a whole. Personally. All of us have different values and morals." He smiled sheepishly and said in a deep Southern accent, "Hey, I'm the chairman. I'm spozed to be listnin' to ya'll."

Morris Williams said he wished he knew what kind of result Mr. Fountain was seeking. "When you come to that kind of drama, an alternative selection for his daughter, maybe."

I gazed up at the stains on the ceiling.

"If the teacher would be glad to do that," Williams continued, "it might take care of the objection right there. The book would remain in place and everyone would walk away happy. That might be a simple solution."

I told the committee about Pittman's refusal to offer alternative texts.

"In that case," William Orr said, "I see no strong reason to eliminate *Lysistrata*. I see none," he said.

"Same here," said Rankin. "You may not agree with it and that's fine."

"Some people won't be satisfied until everything's thrown out," Orr said.

Morris Williams suggested a plain brown paper wrapper. Everyone laughed.

"Shoot," Ellis said, "We're not even going to teach it."

"If it stays in the book, kids'll find it," said Rankin.

Orr waved this away. "If kids find it, let them read it."

Ellis straightened his notes. "So what we're saying is the committee has no objection to leaving *Lysistrata* in the humanities textbook."

"Otherwise they're tying our hands something fierce," said William Orr.

Foreman agreed. "The values far outweigh the faults. Leave it in the book."

Ellis had stronger feelings about "The Miller's Tale." He recommended cutting it out of the book.

Tyre objected. "Another tale could easily be substituted without cutting it out."

"But it's in the book," Ellis said. "Kids would have it."

"If you do that, do you go to the library and throw out all the *Canterbury Tales*?" Tyre asked.

"And the Song of Solomon from the Bible?" Williams added.

Ellis consulted his *Masterplots* notes. "A farcical and bawdy tale."

"That doesn't make it pornographic and obscene," Tyre said. "It makes it crude and rude," Rankin said.

Tyre looked at Rankin. "But there's a difference."

Foreman nodded. "Uh huh, there is."

"The complainant refers to page 213," Ellis said. "When it speaks to discharging gas, Chaucer uses the word 'fart.' And he mentions kissing someone's tail."

"He could've said it worse than that," Foreman said. "The language is supposed to be bawdy. If you read all of the *Canterbury Tales*, this serves a purpose. If you read just this one it becomes bawdy. In the book this is all they consider, but if you're teaching the *Canterbury Tales* it's appropriate."

Ellis returned to his notes. "Chaucer apologized for his vulgarity but used it to depict one of the social types of his day."

"It's one of a series to point up an era," said Foreman. "It covered all of society."

Orr asked if there was another tale they could teach.

"'The Nun's Tale,'" said Rankin. "That's clean."

Ellis sighed. "Why didn't these idiots—Let me ask you this, James Henry Tyre, do you think somewhere the state adoption policy should be mentioned in this report?"

Tyre shrugged. "We have a choice. We can use different materials."

"Or get rid of that curriculum," Ellis suggested again.

"We need to say it's not required reading," Tyre said. "We also need to say how this piece was selected. The student selected the reading, not the teacher. They'll go down and get it at the public library. I checked with the librarian."

"It's true," Foreman said. "*Lysistrata* and "The Miller's Tale" are more frequently requested since the board banned them."

Ellis said he wished someone would ban the history book so his students would read it. They all nodded and laughed. He asked if the committee's recommendation was to leave it in the text.

"Yes," Tyre said, "as an optional selection."

Ellis frowned. "Then how in Sam Hill are you going to

control what they read?"

Rankin suggested simply recommending it not be required.

Orr agreed.

Ellis wanted the report to state clearly that the two works had never been taught. "They're not part of the course."

No one objected. The committee made a few remarks, not all of them flattering, about Reverend Fountain, then they adjourned to eat lunch and write their report.

I drove home elated. Now I just had to make sure the school board followed the committee's recommendation.

The Columbia County school board meets every other Tuesday in the County Commission room overlooking Lake Desoto in the back of the courthouse.

On the night of the April 8 hearing, Susan was outside when I arrived. She introduced me to Monya Virgil, a woman who made me think of Miss Kitty—red hair, tri-colored eye shadow, a beauty mark on her cheek, and a red low-cut ruffled dress (Susan wears skirts and sweaters; I wear jeans or slacks). Monya had moved to Lake City two years before when her husband, Jim, was appointed general manager of the Florida branch of Idaho Timber. They each had a daughter from a previous marriage at Columbia High. Jim's daughter, Laura, planned to take the humanities class in the fall, and Monya's daughter, Erika, planned to take it sometime in the future.

Monya dropped her cigarette on the asphalt and crushed it under her ankle-strap shoe. She blew smoke from her nose. "No preacher will tell *my* kid what to read."

We walked up the stairs to the County Commissioners' room. The windows were open; red-winged blackbirds trilled out by the lake. At seven o'clock, Silas Pittman called the meeting to order. He prayed for the success of the school board and led the small audience in the Pledge of Allegiance. Chairman Dickie Chapple opened the hearing.

I was recognized first. I stood, my hands shaking slightly, and expressed my concern that Pittman's procedure gave board members the power to veto the textbook committee's recommendation when they might not have read the challenged material. I suggested inserting a clause requiring that the board read the books they might ban.

My modest proposal unleashed a roar of resentment. One board member rose out of his chair and shouted at me, "I've been to high school and college and I'm not going to read a book a week!" Haltiwanger and Hudson sided with him. So did Pittman.

After a moment the shouting died down. Dickie Chapple said he didn't have a problem with reading the book. Dianne Lane said she would feel much more comfortable talking to parents if she had read it. She seized the moment to propose a different procedure, one that offered alternative texts.

Once again, Pittman raised the spectre of angry parents demanding creationist texts. No one on the board said a word about Lane's proposal so they went back to mine. Board attorney, Terry McDavid, objected to the clause I'd proposed. Board members could not be required to read challenged books because it would be impossible to prove if they'd read them or not.

I protested, but Keith Hudson cut me off with a motion to approve Pittman's procedure the way it was written. Roger seconded quickly. Haltiwanger and Chappel voted yes, Lane voted no. The motion carried four to one. The hearing was closed. One of the members stood up, turned around, and in the baldest body language I have witnessed to date, scratched his backside.

Susan and Monya and I stood and filed out of the room. As we did, I heard Little whisper, "Who *was* that woman?"

Two weeks later, at the April 22 school board meeting, Silas Pittman read the recommendation of the textbook committee, beginning with *Lysistrata*: "The Committee recognizes that this passage is included in the textbook, but is not required reading for the course. The Committee has no objection to *Lysistrata* remaining as part of the humanities textbook."

The committee's recommendation for "The Miller's Tale" was slightly different: "The Committee recognizes that this passage is included in the textbook, but is not required reading for the course. The Committee has no objection to "The Miller's Tale" remaining as part of the humanities textbook; however, the Committee feels it would be inappropriate to add this selection as a required reading in the course."

Pittman said he agreed with the committee's findings, however, he "felt like that" any literature that took the Lord's name in vain was not appropriate for use in the classroom. He recommended that the board edit out the two classics or ban the book altogether.

Jack Haltiwanger moved to accept Pittman's recommendation, seconded by Dianne Lane. The vote was unanimous.

Reverend Fountain stood and thanked the board for their action.

The following day, all copies of Volume I of the humanities textbook were confiscated and locked in the book room out at the high school.

Three.

When our eight-year-old, Anne, saw the headline the following day—LITERARY CLASSICS ARE CENSORED AT CHS—she burst into tears. "Does that mean they'll come into our house and take all our books?"

"Oh, no, sweetheart," I said, but I could have used a good cry myself.

Ormond tried to console me with a quotation from Twain, usually a great consolation: "First God created idiots. That was for practice. Then he created school boards."

Unconsoled, I read the article on the front page, my first encounter with censorship doubletalk:

> "I do not feel they are appropriate," Superintendent of Schools Silas Pittman told school board members. 'They should be edited out.'
>
> "I concur with the committee's findings they are not appropriate translations for 11th and 12th graders," he added.

I tossed the paper aside. "That is *not* what the committee decided. They recommended that *Lysistrata* or 'The Miller's Tale' *remain* in the textbook but not be required."

"I guess God created superintendents last," Ormond said.

The telephone rang. Muttering "lies and distortions" I went to answer. It was Ed Montgomery, shocked by the school board's decision. He apologized for underestimating what they would do.

"Overestimating," I said.

He asked how I was doing. I said I'd been better.

Later that day, Susan and Monya and I met to decide what to do. We'd been steamrolled at the April 8 meeting. We were women, outsiders, two strikes against us in the eyes of the board.

"But," Monya said, "they're elected."

We decided there was only one way to get Chaucer and Aristophanes back in the classroom: build a coalition of voters to protest the ban. Pack the next meeting. Change the board's narrow mind.

For the next few days we talked to people in town who, like Ed, were shocked by the ban. We asked if they would stand up with us at the next school board meeting. Everyone but my two closest friends, Sharon Richards and Jan King, declined. Teachers were convinced that Pittman would cancel their contract. Anne's elementary school librarian said she and other librarians in town were disturbed by the ban but they, too, were worried about economic reprisal. Instead of speaking out, she planned to offer an in-service day for teachers and librarians about intellectual freedom.

One owner of a local store was offended by the board's action but he feared fundamentalist boycotts if he voiced his opinion. The wife of a prominent businessman in town buttonholed me at Eckerd's and said she and her friends were embarrassed that the school board had censored "The Miller's Tale" and *Lysistrata*. When I asked if she'd say so in public, she said, "Oh, no, my husband won't let me." Our pediatrician's wife—one of the more enlightened people in town—said she disagreed with the board but didn't feel free to say so. "Several board members bring their children to us." Even Lake City Community College declined to take a stand on the issue.

One day over coffee, Susan ruefully summed up the reaction: "Short of doing something, what can we do?"

And that, we assumed, was the end of the story. Without the support of other voters in town, Chaucer and Aristophanes were locked up for good.

There was freedom for me in this act of repression. Since

Ormond and I had arrived in Lake City, I had been screaming, "I can't breathe the *air*," but atmosphere is hard to pin down and this created tension between us.

On good days Ormond was sympathetic—he could see it was a tough place to live. On bad days he was angry, impatient—these were good people, the salt of the earth, the *folk*, for Christ's sake. I could be happy if I only tried harder.

God, God, I do love this man but there are days I could shoot him and walk away smiling.

For six years I had tried to be happy. I kept a list of the things that I liked about life in Lake City, a secular version of counting my blessings: our house on Hernando, the magnolia out front that the kids loved to climb; the sand pear out back that they gleaned every summer to raise extra money, three pears for a quarter. I liked our neighbors, our dentist, our pediatrician, the guys down at Goodyear, and our dear friends, the Richards and Kings. I liked the cool clear days in December, the abundance of parking, the Christmas parade down Marion Street— floats pulled by teenage boys in their pickups, their windows rolled down so they could toss candy to kids or some girl who slid her hand through the air and murmured, "Hey, Willie."

My favorite place was Lake City Pharmacy overlooking the square. The owner, Billy Ogden, was the third generation to own this family business, a long narrow store plowed by three rows of shelves—athletic supporters not all that far from Whitman's Samplers—and a fountain where the kids and I often sat at the scarred orange counter with an ice cream or coke for thirty-five cents while Billy filled our prescription. He knew his place was unique, but just in case someone suspected he didn't, he kept a quote from *The New Yorker* taped to his cash register—Simone de Beauvoir lamenting the passing of the old-fashioned drugstore (Lake City Pharmacy, too, has since passed; Billy now fills prescriptions at K-Mart.)

The morning after the school board banned the humanities textbook, I liked the place even more. I was sitting at the counter with a twenty-five cent cup of coffee when Billy sidled up and sat on the stool next to mine. He leaned his curly head toward me and said, *sotto voce*, "Does this mean I can't read my *Playboy*?"

I liked all of this about life in Lake City but I couldn't imagine calling it home. There were days I considered this a personal failure. There were days I felt crazy, saw myself in the future, the Woman Who Never Adjusted, the madwoman in the attic of our house on Hernando, like Agnes in Albee's *Delicate Balance*, mad as a hatter, my mouth full of ribbons.

But on April 22, 1986, the day the board banned the book, these feelings faded. I had something concrete to point to, a manifestation of an atmosphere I couldn't pin down. I could now say to Ormond, "Here, look at this. This is what I've been talking about." It was like a reprieve; I wasn't crazy. I was, to quote Stoppard, "stark raving sane."

I finished chapter three of the novel and took it to Tallahassee for Jerry Stern's novel workshop. Before the seminar started, we talked about the ban in Lake City. A colleague, Joe Straub, gave me a copy of Vonnegut's essay, "Palm Sunday." Some colleagues looked on the bright side—banning was great box office for books. Most were baffled by the decision to ban—surely there were dirtier words on the walls of the high school. "That isn't the classroom," Jerry observed. "Some people think the classroom is an incubator—it has to be pure or the students will die."

We moved on to fiction. Jerry liked most of my chapter but he thought the character of the producer was too flat—"sleep city." He was right. I was trying to sneak *The Catlins'* producer, Chris McIntyre, onto the page, but he was, at his most interesting, a thin ineffectual man with strands of blond hair combed back over a bald spot.

Jerry suggested creating a character slightly offbeat, more artistic, someone who gets media attention but nothing more mainstream than *Interview*.

I said, "What's *Interview*?"

I picked up a copy and read it before I drove home, then, in the car, I mulled it all over. Somewhere between Tallahassee and Lake City, the alchemy of the creative process combined what I knew about folklore and film, and a new character appeared in my mind. Driving east on I-10, I knew how he looked; how he drove, on I-85:

Andrej Pysanky, the Ukrainian master of black and white cinema, hailed internationally as the Man of Monochrome, three-time winner of the *Palm d'Or*, was driving Roz Lawson, the failed playwright of Ohumpka, Florida, to the Hartsfield Atlanta International Airport.

She glanced at Pysanky. At yesterday's screening of *Heart's Curtain* he'd reminded her of Truffaut—the same kind of eyes, the same shaggy gray hair—but now, sitting so close to her in his Kharmann Ghia, he seemed smaller, more fragile. Maybe it was the way he drove, his shoulders hunched forward, his hands gripping the wheel, his gray eyes fixed on the road up ahead. She had no idea how long he'd been in this country, but he drove like a newcomer, a Displaced Person, a man with a learner's permit, barely breaking forty-five, apparently oblivious to the morning rush-hour traffic that parted and swept around him.

The scene continued to take shape. *Pysanky*, I knew, was the art of decorating Ukrainian eggs; Ormond and the children and I had watched a woman in White Springs performing the process.

Pysanky looked over at Roz. "How is it you know about *pysanky*?"

"My husband's a folklorist."

"That is nice. I like flowers."

He told her about growing up in the Ukraine. His mother was famous for her *pysanky*. When he was a boy, he watched her by the hour, heating the beeswax, drawing designs with the *kistka*, dying the egg, color by color, the lightest one first. It took his mother eight or nine hours to finish one egg.

He took the name Pysanky as a young man in Paris because the word summed up his philosophy of art. "It was in this way that I used to make films. Slowly. Putting layer on layer. But they do not want

this film anymore. They want now cars chasing over
each other. That is why I am making *Heart's Curtain*.
American soap opera is slow, like *pysanky*. The stories are layered, one on each other."

Roz felt a new rise in interest; she had never
thought of soap opera that way.

Neither had I. I'd been trying to make *Heart's Curtain* in
The Catlins' image—bad and low budget. Now I saw how good
it could be in the hands of a man like Pysanky—low-budget,
yes, but offbeat and brooding, shot in black and white—in short,
art soap, an oxymoron if ever I'd heard one, a crazy juxtaposi-
tion I thought could only occur in a novel. Three years later
Lynch gave us *Twin Peaks*.

The writing went well for the next couple of weeks. I
revised chapter three and began chapter four. One morning in
early May the telephone rang. It was Rutledge Liles, a member
of the Board of Governors of the Florida Bar Association. He had
seen my name in Jacksonville's *Florida Times Union* and he
wanted me to join a PBS panel, "The First Amendment in the
Classroom," for the bicentennial of the Constitution. I accepted.
Before hanging up, he commiserated about the board banning
the textbook. He was surprised the A.C.L.U. wasn't involved.

I didn't tell Mr. Liles that the American Civil Liberties
Union had not crossed my mind.

There is no listing for the A.C.L.U. in the Lake City phone
book. I called the Gainesville chapter which referred me to Steve
Forester, legal director of the A.C.L.U. Foundation of Florida in
South Miami.

After listening to me for almost a hour, Forester said we
might well have a case. The board had, in his opinion, violated
our children's constitutional right to receive information pro-
tected under the First Amendment. He advised us, however, to
write Pittman and ask him to urge the board to rescind its
decision. Forester said he would be sending a similar letter.

Writers have been favorite targets of school boards and so,
understandably, school boards are favorite targets of writers. I
already knew Mark Twain's opinion. Kurt Vonnegut wasn't

much kinder. He wrote the essay "Palm Sunday" after a North Dakota school board burned *Slaughterhouse Five*:

> Such lunks are often the backbone of volunteer fire departments and the United States Infantry and cake sales and so on, and they have been thanked often enough for that. But they have no business supervising the educations of children in a free society. They are just too bloody stupid.

He made several high-minded statements about books and freedom that Monya and Susan and I shamelessly cribbed for our letter to Pittman (we put ourselves in Vonnegut's place and decided he wouldn't mind):

> We believe that books are sacred to free men and women, that wars have been fought against nations which object to books and censor them, and that, if you are an American, you must allow all ideas—even those you may dislike—to circulate freely.

We added a few concerns of our own:

> We believe that your attempt to shield our children from what you have deemed "unacceptable reading material" limits their education and deprives them of a crucial opportunity to read and evaluate material on their own.

Finally, we told Pittman we had contacted the American Civil Liberties Union but we would only file a complaint if the board refused to rescind its decision.

Susan delivered the letter in person to Pittman who answered the following day:

> This is to advise that your letter of May 12, 1986, was received in the County School Board Office too late to be adendad [sic] for the May 13th meeting and will therefore be agendad for May 27, 1986.

She also delivered copies of our letter to the *Lake City Reporter* and the local radio station, WGRO. John Hindson, the British disk jockey (as small towns would have it, our pediatrician's wife's brother-in-law), read the letter on the air. The next day the *Lake City Reporter* carried the headline: ACLU MAY BE CALLED INTO BOOK-CENSOR CASE.

There is nothing like the threat of an A.C.L.U. lawsuit to stir up a small Southern town. In the two weeks before the next school board meeting, all hell broke loose. Ray Callahan—an appliance repairman and school board aspirant—warned listeners on "Speak Out" that the A.C.L.U. was "a bunch of weirdoes and queers and homosexuals." His homophobia surfaced a few days later in a letter in the *Lake City Reporter*:

> It seems that three women, Monya Virgil, Susan Davis and Claudia Johnson, are unhappy about the censoring of offensive material ... Maybe the three women wouldn't mind if homosexuals taught their children. If that is the case, I would suggest that they live in San Francisco.

The *Reporter* ran its own editorial accusing "supposedly responsible school board members and supposedly well-educated school administrators" of buckling under to a "vocal minority of bluenoses who would have us return to the days of book-burning" and who have "set the stage once again for Columbia County to be held up to ridicule ... We are not talking about pornography here, but textbooks approved by the Florida Department of Education."

An unprecedented number of callers responded to the question in the Reporter's daily feature, "Columbia Consensus":

> Do you think two books should have been
> censored at Columbia High School?
> YES 74%   NO 26%
> (76 responses)

Yes, we need to train our children in the right way. Yes, they should be banned and also the three people who are protesting censorship. Yes, we don't need to teach our children filth and garbage in the schools. They get enough of it elsewhere. Yes, let's return to the moral standards our nation was founded upon. Yes, I don't want those three ladies dumping their garbage and trash on me. We have rights, too, Pastor fountain stands tall. Yes, and we wonder what's wrong with our youth. Yes, we don't need those kinds of books on our shelves and at the library. Yes, they get enough pornography at the newsstands. Yes, I believe the school board was open-minded. As a Christian I feel other Christians should be 100 percent behind them. No, those bozos shouldn't be censoring our literature. No, it's everybody's right to read classics and it's embarrassing to live in a community where they were censored. No, and I admire the women who filed the lawsuit. No, but here we go again. The ACLU and all holyrollers are going to come out of the woodwork, and the sad thing is that 95 percent of the conversation will be over the heads of 95 percent of the people of Columbia County, but it's gonna be fun .... .

Steve Forester's letter to Pittman arrived on May 22. The board's decision to ban "The Miller's Tale" and *Lysistrata* was made, Forester wrote, "in apparent ignorance of the works themselves, their universally recognized literary and cultural merit, and most importantly the First Amendment values at stake. We are prepared to sue you and the Board unless the Board rescinds its unconstitutional action."

In the midst of all this, Sharon Saunders, a calm black reporter who had cover the story from the beginning, decided to drive out to the high school and talk to those most affected by the board's decision to ban the humanities book, Every student Saunders talked to said the board shouldn't have done it.

"It wasn't saying anything that bad," said Mary Lee, as senior. "There was nothing in the play that I didn't already know about."

Sarah Cheryan, a senior, agreed, "Once you see the moral to the story you can put everything else aside."

Aggie Fulcher told Sounders she enjoyed *Lysytrata*. "It was a good play. Most of the kids laughed at it and wanted to read it again."

So did dozens of other people in town. For two weeks, to the dismay of the censors, *Lysistrata* and "The Miller's Tale" enjoyed a renaissance in Lake City. The public librarian, Eileen Brunner, said both works, rarely checked out, were in great demand. John Hindson had a wonderful time at WGRO station reading excerpts from both banned classics aloud on the air. (He received one death threat by chose to ignore it.)

"I read what I thought were the filthiest bits," he gleefully told the St Petersburg Times. "Nobody in Lake City would dream of reading it in the first place, and all of a sudden, everyone was reading it."

And more people than usual, I suspect, were listening to "Speak Out" on May 26, the eve of the big school board meeting. Monya and Susan and I got together with a bottle of wine and tuned in to listen. Bob Murray kicked off the show by praising "the three ladies" for taking "the politically unpopular position of fighting the school board." He hoped the board didn't "get macho and decide not to change their opinion, because it will be very very costly and I personally believe they're gonna lose."

The first caller was John Hindson, who chastised Ray Callahan for his remarks about homosexuals. "If Mr. Callahan wants to debate homosexuality, I'd be very happy to do it with him any time, but the issue here is censorship, and I just wish he'd call in tonight with his views on that and not his views on other people's lifestyles."

The next caller didn't identify himself, but the voice sounded familiar. "I'd like to just say that I'm glad someone in our community is standing up for the Constitution and I think the school board was wrong in censoring those works."

I smiled at Susan and Monya. The caller was Ormond.

Four.

Tuesday, May 27, dawned hot and hazy.

Dianne Lane met with Susan and Monya and me one last time in hopes of avoiding a lawsuit. She admitted that the school board had made a terrible mistake by not following its own textbook committee's recommendation, but she thought she had a solution: she would ask her colleagues to return the humanities text to the classroom for the remaining five days of school and choose a different text for the fall. We weren't crazy about the idea of changing the text but we conceded if the board approved her proposal, the threat of a lawsuit would pass.

That night, the board room was packed, but not with people who wanted the board to rescind its decision. Jim Virgil wanted to speak on our behalf so the school board might realize there were more than "three ladies" opposed to the ban. He was the only person on the agenda to defend the humanities textbook.

The board sat at their semicircular promontory at the south end of the room—Little, Hudson, Haltiwanger, Chapple; Pittman sat between Dianne Lane and board attorney, Terry McDavid. He opened the meeting with a prayer and the Pledge of Allegiance, then Chairman Chapple gave Jim Virgil the floor.

Jim introduced himself, carefully laying out his credentials: a bachelor of arts from Purdue, a doctor of jurisprudence from the University of Notre Dame, general manager of Idaho Timber, a Columbia County based business with annual sales in excess of twenty million dollars, and the father of two daughters at Columbia County High. He did this "to dispel any notion that he was some dang liberal from Massachusetts who came slithering into our community to tell you how to run our city."

I pretended this reference to slithering liberals was a rhetorical ploy, "common ground," as Jessie Jackson would say two years later, but I knew it was not; censorship makes strange bedfellows.

Jim reminded the board of the greatness of the literature in question. He pointed out to the board that the Lord whose name was taken in vain in *Lysistrata* was probably Zeus so Christians need not be offended. The board, he said, had been inconsistent in banning the humanities text but allowing the English textbook—*Adventure in Appreciation*—to remain. He called the board's attention to page 218 where Steinbeck took the *real* Lord's name in vain, and reminded the board that Whitman and Poe were also included when it was a well-known fact that Whitman was a homosexual (Jim looked straight at Ray Callahan when he said this) and that Edgar Allen Poe had married his thirteen-year-old first cousin which made him guilty of incest in forty or fifty states in this Union.

"Who are you protecting by banning this book?" Virgil asked. "You are protecting Columbia County High School seniors. A year from now they will be college students, they will be in the armed forces, they'll be working in factories, they'll be registered voters, and if you think by banning this book because it takes the Lord's name in vain you're protecting them—adults already or almost adults—you do them an injustice. There is worse language than is contained in this book on almost every overpass on I-75 from Flint, Michigan to Naples, Florida."

He recommended challenging the text at the state level to spare the Columbia County taxpayers the cost of a suit as well as the ridicule that would be heaped on them by surrounding counties and towns. "My daughter has stated to me that in several of her classrooms, at least two or three, they have as standard equipment in the classroom—buckets—so when a hard rain comes they can catch the rain from the leaking roof with the buckets. I suggest to you gentlemen that you save our money, reverse this decision, and fix the leaky roof at the high school. Thank you very much." He sat down to sparse applause.

Chapple recognized the Reverend Fritz Fountain, a pale,

pudgy, middle-aged man whose black hair, suit, and glasses seemed all of a piece.

"I'm Dr. Fritz Fountain," he said in a deep nasal drawl. "I'm a licensed marriage and family therapist in private practice. I'm a veteran of twenty-two years in the public school system, a great many of those spent in Columbia County, and I am a parent. According to the newspaper, I am a fanatical Southern Baptist. Now, that just gives you my credentials.

"This whole escapade began when I picked up a request form for the examination of school media and filled that out on a couple of passages which I felt was not appropriate reading in the public school system, especially since, as I stated in my last statement before the board, this same language used in the hallway would probably merit a suspension from school. Now let me go on to say that I agree with Mr. Virgil that we could probably see things much worse than this on the men's room wall, but the men's room wall is not required reading—"

Jim said, "Neither is the humanities textbook."

Fountain ignored him. "Now, reading in the newspaper, I have been equated with Adolf Hitler as a book burner, and to be classified with Hitler is certainly something that I do not appreciate because I'm not a book burner.

"But to carry this still further, let me suggest to the media that Hitler was also a writer and in his major work, *Mein Kampf,* he wrote some of the most outrageously racist comments that were ever written which proves that everything you see in print is not true. Mussolini was a newspaper editor, so was Lenin and so was Stalin, and each used the printed word to vilify, to libel, to defame, to traduce, and to calumniate anyone that they wanted to deal with, anyone they thought was a threat to their authority, their position, so that those who had the initial courage to speak would somehow crawl away in the woodwork and never speak again. And I leave it to the board and to the board's consideration and to those assembled here to decide such tactics could and are being practiced in the United States today.

"I've been told that these two works are classics. And I have heard this applied to them many times, and I will agree. But sometimes this seems to me to be classified as a classic approaches role of biblical canonicity. Once you make it, it can never be taken away. And if something goes on that list, it can never be removed. Well, I'm going to have to step into the line of children's classics to give you an example.

"Several years ago when I was in elementary school there was a story that was a children's classic called *Little Black Sambo*. Not long ago I am told that because of the racist content of that book—and I will agree it is very racist—someone came along and said this should be removed because it says derogatory things about the black race. And that classic was taken off the list. And I have to admit that gave me courage to say that the kind of language that is used here is not used in a regular way in my home. And I do not appreciate my daughter being exposed to it in a public school classroom and I think this board agrees from the action they have already taken. I have not said to these ladies that they can't buy this book or that they cannot check it out of the public library and read it themselves. I am just simply saying that according to the United States Supreme Court where they said first of all that school system basically belongs to each of us and we have a requirement to the school system even if we do not have children who go to that school system because we all benefit from what they learn in school.

"To say that a child's mind will not be changed by what they read is to hit at the very framework of public education. Why do we take them into the classroom? Why do we require them to read? If it will not change their minds, if it will not change their thoughts? And so what we're saying, if they read the baser, they approach the baser."

Chaucer and Aristophanes, baser? I thought.

"If they read the higher, they approach the higher. For one is the sum total of all of his experiences."

Fountain congratulated the board for banning the text and sat down to booming applause.

Chapple recognized Ray Callahan, who flabbergasted everyone in the room by asking the board to rescind its decision. His reasons, however, were different from ours.

"As far as the A.C.L.U. goes, I really believe we should be cautious about letting them get a foothold in Columbia County. I've made a statement on the radio station—I was pretty hot, maybe some of the people here heard it; sometimes you got to eat a little crow so I'll eat a little—but I made a statement that the A.C.L.U. is made up of weirdoes and freaks. If you watched *Good Morning America* this morning just before eight o'clock— all this week they're doing a study on pornography, hard core pornography, the kind you wouldn't want anybody to see, uh, there's nothing good in that stuff, and there was one lady with the pornography commission, the anti-pornography commission, she was stating how there were direct links to pornography with violent sexual acts, these are known facts, the A.C.L.U. guy got up and said there's never been any proof that pornographic material has had any effect on people who have read them. Any adverse effect. I can tell you that isn't true because it isn't for myself, but I'm not going to go into that now.

"If any of you watch TV for any length of time, you'd notice that many of the A.C.L.U. people, the lawyers, attorneys, are fighting gay rights issues, I believe it's Collier County, they no longer have a baccalaureate service because of the A.C.L.U.— I tell you, you don't want these folks in your town, they're bad news, they're real bad news. So I have to ask you to reconsider, very seriously consider what this means.

"I would like to know what right these three ladies have to tell me as a parent that my children must read this type of material, or necessarily not read it but be subjected to it in the school system. State sanctioned. I'm pretty upset about that. I don't allow my children to use profound [sic] language at home. If I find out they're using it, they're disciplined sternly. I do not allow my children to use sexually explicit literature. Granted they're very young, six and eight years old, but they're already beginning to learn about sex in their own home. And they're learning the correct way. But I will not allow it. Now granted you can't stop it for everybody. They're going to hear it on the school bus, there's nothing you can do to stop that. But, for God's sake," he shouted, unaware that he was taking the Lord's name in vain, "you can't state sanction profanity!

"Tonight, you essentially have two choices," he said, calming down. "One, fight the issue. If you fight the issue, you must be prepared to stand by your decision, regardless of the outcome. And quite frankly, it's a no-win situation. The other choice, you know in life, sometimes we have to compromise. Sometimes we have to back up and punt. The other possibility that you have is to go ahead and put the humanities text back in the classroom. This should satisfy these three ladies and the A.C.L.U., and then this summer—I understand this book is under review, right?"

"One more year," Dianne Lane said.

"One more year. I would suggest that we, that the board begin to express the concerns that you have to the state of books that have this type of language in it, the man mentioned," Callahan gestured toward Jim Virgil, "that there are other books that have foul language in them, I think we need, ya'll need, to address this situation at the state level and ask them if they could remove the offensive literature. I understand that these two particular works, that one of them at least is a very bad translation, maybe another translation would be acceptable. I haven't read it and I don't intend to read it. I see enough trash every day. As the man says," again he gestured toward Jim, "you can walk down the highway and see enough stuff as it is. I feel at this time, as much as I hate saying it, that the only option this board really has, unless you intend to spend a whole lot of money, is to go ahead and put the book back in, but I don't like saying that because I agree with your decision, but I think that's the only decision you've got. And then petition the state for a book that's more acceptable to this group here."

Ray Callahan returned to his seat to scattered applause.

The last person to address the board was Wilbur Lloyd, an old-timer notorious in town for filibustering "Speak Out." He warmed up to the issue at hand by claiming there wasn't "a soul in the room who was within fifteen years" of his age, then he launched a long narrative reminiscent of Twain's great digressions:

"Now this movement here, in this last few years in Columbia County—I don't know nothing about nowhere else, I don't have a car, couldn't drive one if I did have one, my wife's an invalid so therefore don't need no car—so I don't need to be running here there and about. All I can keep up with is what it's been like in the last five years. But it started a little further back than that. It really started in 1964. Seventy-five percent of you people wasn't here at that time. I told them right out there in the middle of that park in 1964 that I knew where nine old white whore houses were at in Lake City—if you'll pardon the expression."

There was a startled silence followed by titters as the crowd realized that Wilbur Lloyd was rambling on about brothels in an effort to ban bawdy classics.

"There was eight gambling joints and a moonshine still," Lloyd continued, "every five miles from the county line, thank you gentlemen, if you call yourselves gentlemen (laughter) and if you don't believe me carry me out there, I'll show 'em to you. One of them's over on here on main street two or three blocks from here, two stories high, seventy-five rooms, I know because I went up there once or twice."

Embarrassed laughter again.

"I live all these years and I've done everything in the world: I've sold moonshine, I've made moonshine, I've served five months in the Duvall County jail for selling moonshine, but since nineteen hundred and fifty one and even before then when I was in the legislature, these people that's old enough to remember will remember that I never did promise anything that I was gonna do that I didn't do, and I never did been called a lawyer, and I never been accused of taking a bribe in all these years."

Eventually he sneaked up on what we guessed was his point: "If we're gonna be done like we been done in the last few years around here by a bunch of communistic atheistic ignoramuses come a busting in here from somewhere and suing the county and jumping on the school board and having us having to pay for it, I say don't leave it up to the taxpayer, but I say this gentlemen and I'm going to hush. If they put it out there in the school and you don't want your child to take it, if enough of you will back me, she won't have to take it. I have seen the time when people would give from sundown the next evening to leave town if they left at five o'clock the next morning. I been here. And I ain't a bit too good to start a movement and lead a movement of that kind. I know if I had a daughter I'd put her in a private school before I'd let her go with anything like that, what's in that book. And if you all will come over when I put this all together and see that you feel just like I do. If you don't, you're not an old time George Washington Patrick Henry Southern cracker. Thank you."

"Thank you, Mr. Lloyd," sighed Dickie Chapple.

The audience coughed and shuffled. Jack Haltiwanger leaned toward his microphone. "I don't have a doctor's degree"—a clear reference to me, but then, Don Caldwell had tried to warn me—"but I do have a master's degree plus twenty something hours, and I've had an opportunity, contrary to what the paper said, to take some humanities courses and also read this book here. And four years ago people elected me to this office, I committed myself to vote the way I thought was best for the boys and girls. Therefore, Mr. Chairman, I stick with my decision. I don't like the idea of spending money on a suit, but we have morals to stand up to."

Hudson and Little concurred to wild applause.

When the room became quiet again, Dianne Lane leaned forward and said, "We are faced with an imminent lawsuit. I was hoping to avoid a lawsuit by finding some common ground, perhaps we could compromise. I spent a lot of time today talking to Mrs. Davis and Mrs. Johnson trying to find out where we could possibly find something to agree on. One of their major complaints, I think, is that we did go against the textbook committee's recommendation without going through the same process we require them to go through. And I can understand and agree with that point. I think the committee made a responsible recommendation and maybe we made a mistake in not upholding it.

"I think if—and we've already agreed that we're looking for a new humanities book—if we reconsider our decision which was based on Dr. Pittman's recommendation that we go against the textbook committee's recommendation, we leave the books in the classroom for the next week, I think that we might possibly avert the lawsuit, and I think Lake City deserves not to have to pay for this kind of lawsuit if we can possibly compromise somewhere."

Haltiwanger objected, "The translations that I read, I wouldn't want them being taught."

"I wouldn't either," Lane said. "I think we're all agreed

about that. I think *Lysistrata* in the translation it's in has lost everything it became classic for."

Haltiwanger agreed. "That's why Dr. Pittman made his recommendation."

"I understand why he made his objection," Lane said, "but if we sincerely want to avert a lawsuit and it's already agreed we'll look for another humanities book, what can the harm be putting them back in the classroom and not teaching these two for the rest of the school year? We're going to have new books by next year."

"Mr. Chairman, Dr. Pittman," said Roger Little, "we took some pretty severe tongue-lashing in the last thirty minutes and thirty days I like to ever get—"

Pittman didn't let Little finish. "I think I would feel differently if this was a library book. If this were a library book, where students and parents could make a determination whether or not they wanted to go and check this book out and read it. I think it's a different situation completely when this board has to approve curriculum and approves material of that nature."

"I *agree* with you," Lane insisted. "I really hate to have this in the classroom. But I think we have to back up. And we've already agreed to look for an alternative humanities book."

Pittman shook his head. He saw no good reason for compromising his principles for one week. "I might would have felt differently about this a week ago, but I went back one more time and read it word for word, I took time on a Saturday morning and I read it word for word and I'm even *more* convinced, not just for the reason I had mentioned before now, but for *other* reasons. I don't think this should be required as far as the curriculum is concerned. That's just my opinion."

Lane nodded. "I agree, it is a crude translation—"

"*Super* crude," Pittman said.

"—and whether we're talking about a monotheistic or a pantheistic type religion, when someone says 'Oh, God,' I can't help but agree with Dr. Pittman that they are invoking the one Supreme God. And I agree with him that they have taken poetic license. But I still think we should compromise."

Chapple looked right and left. "Any board member want to change his decision?"

Lane made one more plea. "We've already made it clear that we're going to be looking for a new humanities book for next year. But I don't think that they will back down because they think we have violated their children's constitutional right by censoring these works and unless we back up to the point that we accept the textbook committee's recommendation, I know the wheels are going to start turning."

Hudson said, "Let 'em roll."

Five.

After the board voted four to one to keep Chaucer and Aristophanes locked up in the book room, Lake City became laughingstock.

"Vulgar language?" wrote the columnist Buddy Davis in the *Gainesville Sun*:

> My version of "The Miller's Tale" contains the word "ass," featured no fewer than 13 times in Holy Writ, referred to a beast of burden thought so stupid that kissing it evolved into an insult to human intelligence and the word itself corrupted into a human's behind. My version also contains the word "fart." Could Chaucer be improved by substituting "posterior" and "violent flatulence?" Ridiculous.
>
> If the Rev. Fountain protesteth too much, perhaps it's because Chaucer treats a fellow cleric—the incense bearing church clerk—too irreverently.

An editorial in the *Lake City Reporter* predicted that the ridicule would continue:

> The class of '86 also, just in the last few weeks, has had to put up with a school administration that still censors their reading material and plans to do so by razor-cutting whole stories out of state-approved textbooks.
>
> Apparently, what might be proper for all the

high school students in the other 66 counties of Florida isn't proper for the innocents of Columbia County.

As some of the seniors head to college next year, they may need cotton in their ears to muffle the sounds of their classmates' giggling over that one.

And, finally, we hope the grads of '86 won't be too embarrassed in coming years by any lack of knowledge about the sexual side of life. It seems they graduated from a school system which not only won't allow any reading about sex, but doesn't have any other information that might be called "sex education," either.

Yes, the grads of l986 have their whole lives to look forward to, and tonight they will be filled with pride and anticipation by their speakers.

But they have a lot to look back on, too.

Sure enough, an editorial in the *Tampa Tribune* dismissed Columbia County as a cultural swamp:

Culturally, Columbia County up on Florida's state line apparently lies deeper in the Okefenokee Swamp than its northern end does geographically.

Evidence of this came in the county school board's reaffirmation the other day of an April decision to ban Aristophanes and Geoffrey Chaucer from the high school humanities course.

The present humanities text contains adaptations of the Greek playwright's *Lysistrata* as well as "The Miller's Tale" from Chaucer's *Canterbury Tales*. The board voted to throw out the textbook after a minister complained both works contained obscene language and sexual references.

The two classics were zilch insofar as the board was concerned. The most moderate position was that of school board member Dianne Lamb [sic], who agreed to switching to another textbook this fall but didn't think the current text should be withdrawn for the remaining few weeks of the present term ... Anyway, in today's era of the sexual revolution, and only a year or so before they can vote, join the military forces, and enter college or the world of work, Columbia County High School students are scarcely going to encounter anything new to them in Aristophanes or Chaucer.

It may not even be new to them that along with the alligators and water moccasins, a lot of jackasses inhabit the reaches of the Okefenokee.

I found satisfaction in this widespread guffaw, a fine and funny poetic justice. My rage was replaced, at least for the moment, by rich delight at the ridicule the censors had heaped on themselves: the comic spirit they had tried to suppress had come back to haunt them. I knew Chaucer and Aristophanes would be enjoying it, too: Aristophanes adding school board members to the others he blasts in *The Birds*; Chaucer penning a tale about superintendents. My mother sent me a quote from Sean O'Casey that I taped over my desk, a passage about laughter being "wine for the soul ... brought in to mock at things as they are so that they may topple down, and make room for better things to come." Beside it I taped a speech from *Lysistrata* spoken by the chorus of old women. On the eve of three women suing the superintendent and school board, the passage seemed perfect for Pittman:

> It may be hard, you silly old ass
> But who brought you to this stupid pass?

Local reactions were different.

The very Reverend Fritz Fountain stated he was sorry local action was necessary to clean up the textbook, but the state should never have approved the text in the first place. "I'm proud that our school board had the courage to correct the mistake," he told the *Lake City Reporter*.

Letters defending the board peppered the editorial page:

> Khrushchev, leader of the Communist party in

Russia in the 1950s and early '60s, said we (America) would destroy ourselves from within. The liberal-minded people of our county are coming [sic] their best to make a prophet out of him! Hooray for our school board.

The Beulah Baptist Association wrote to the board, proving once again that reading a book is not a prerequisite for banning:

> On behalf of the twenty-eight Southern Baptist Churches of the Beulah Baptist Association, with 8,928 members, the Executive Committee voted unanimously to commend you for your wise decision to remove the distasteful literature from our students [sic] curriculum. We know that you have been sharply criticized by a small vocal minority, but rest assured that the large silent majority appreciate your stand.
>
> Please know that many of us are praying that God's wisdom will be yours in the heavy responsibility that is yours.

When the *Reporter* printed the letter, several Baptists complained that the letter did not, in fact, represent their opinion. Beulah's director of missions, Jerry Adkins, conceded he only reflected the opinion of ninety percent.

Monya and Susan and I received a spate of angry calls from people demanding to know why we wanted "that filth" in the classroom. Monya saw these calls as a challenge, disarming more than one anonymous caller with her cheerful discussion. She changed more than one mind. Susan and I were less sanguine. Ormond was weary. "Look," he said to some angry man late one night, "I didn't ask for this call."

Don Caldwell invited us to his office at the *Lake City Reporter*. He felt obliged to warn us that we had graduated, in the minds of a good many people in town, from "the three ladies" to "prostitutes" and "filthy liberals," the last a real laugh considering Susan and Monya were consummate conservatives.

But more people than ever were stopping us at the Post Office or the produce section of Publix to express their support, though they still refused to say so in public. The next time I took Anne and Ross to our pediatrician, his wife summoned me into a private office and said that she wanted to join the A.C.L.U.

I called Steve Forester, who asked for transcripts of the meeting on May 27. He said he would start searching for an attorney to represent us. Susan picked up the tape of the meeting at the school board building; I transcribed it—chuckling as I listened to Ray Callahan repeatedly take the Lord's name in vain ("For God's sake! You can't state-sanction profanity!")—and Monya made copies, a division of labor that lasted throughout the case. We pooled our money for postage and sent the transcript down to Miami.

Forester called two days later to say that Sam Jacobson might take the case. A graduate of Duke law school, Jacobson is a senior partner in the Jacksonville law firm, Datz, Jacobson & Lembcke, and a fierce proponent of the First Amendment. In 1971 he had argued a vagrancy case with First Amendment elements before the Supreme Court. His victory—announced on the front page of the February 25, 1972 *New York Times*, next to a photograph of Nixon touring Peking—rendered vagrancy laws in this country unconstitutional.

Jacobson called on June 4. The board's action, he said, was "an act of provincialism that goes to the heart of the First Amendment right to receive information." He was considering taking the case but he wanted to be sure that we understood what we were getting into.

I hadn't fielded questions so hard and fast since I defended my doctoral exams at Florida State: Had we thought of the heat we would get when this went to court? Did we understand that it involved more than putting our name on the complaint? Had we thought it might jeopardize our husbands' employment? Did we realize we would be going back and forth to Jacksonville for the case, that we would probably be cross-examined by school board attorneys? Were we up to that?

I said that we were. Ormond worked for the state, so we felt his job wasn't threatened. As director of the Chamber of

Commerce, Doug Davis had taken some heat from those who thought he should keep his wife quiet, but he told them she had a right to think and say what she wanted. Jim Virgil's job was the most vulnerable (the president of Idaho Timber had fundamentalist leanings); nevertheless, he wanted to join the case as a plaintiff, regardless of consequences. So did Susan, Monya, and I.

"Fine," Jacobson said. He asked for a copy of the censored humanities textbook and any names of high school students who wanted to join us. Susan and Monya and I made some calls and found a few interested students, but their parents would not let them take part in the case.

The rest of the summer was devoted to establishing our legal standing. None of us had children in the humanities class at the time the textbook was banned, but Laura Virgil, Jim's daughter, was signed up for the class in the fall. Her stepsister, Erika, Monya's daughter, was so outraged by the ban she refused to sign up at all, and Susan's tenth-grader, Lee, felt the same way. Ross and Anne were much younger—they'd start kindergarten and fourth grade in the fall—but I wanted to be on the case because I was worried about a growing censorship trend.

I wasn't alone. On July 27, Eva Parziale of the Associated Press ran a story about four major censorship cases plaguing Florida's public schools. Besides our own in Lake City, a Tampa school had suppressed an underground student magazine. In April 1985 the Walton County School Board had removed *Catcher in the Rye* from an 11th grade college-bound English class after a student complained that the book took the Lord's name in vain. In Panama City, located in North Florida Bay County, the school board had created a nine member commission to review all books offered to the system's twenty thousand students. They banned sixty-four books and eventually reinstated sixty-three, refusing to lift the ban on Robert Cormier's young adult novel, *I Am the Cheese*.

There was a similarity in these cases, another facet of censorship double-talk: apparently aware how abhorrent book banning was to some people, superintendents and board members all over Florida were insisting no book had been banned.

"We did not ban the book," said Walton County school

board member, Gary Billingsley, "we removed it from the classroom curriculum."

Bay County Superintendent Leonard Hall echoed this opinion. "There is no censorship. It's simply the responsibility of the school system that materials at the appropriate level and interests of the child are taken care of."

Instigator of the move to ban the Bay County books, Charles E. Collins, told one reporter, "We're not in favor of censorship." His was simply "a group trying to improve the reading quality in the classroom."

And Silas Pittman flatly denied that censorship had occurred in Columbia County. Thrice approved by state educators and used for six years at Columbia High, the humanities textbook had not been banned when the board locked it up in the book room. This was "selection"—not censorship—because a school board, Pittman insisted, has absolute jurisdiction over curriculum.

I put my novel away for the summer, wisdom born of previous summers when I had tried to write and take care of the children and neither went well. I would return to the novel in August when Anne entered fourth grade and Ross would begin kindergarten.

I helped them pick sand pears and build a small stand to sell them out in front of our house. We read all three Pippi Longstocking books and wished there were more. Ormond and I took them with us to Orlando for the PBS panel I'd been invited to join. We drove down the evening before and went for a swim (the Marriott boasted the world's largest pool). Ormond insisted a short dark man in the water with his son was Geraldo Rivera.

"Don't be silly," I said.

The next day Rivera sat four seats away from me on the panel.

Directly across sat U.S. District Judge W. Brevard Hand, who was preparing to hear a censorship case in Alabama where fundamentalist parents wanted forty-five textbooks banned from the schools because they promoted the "religion" of secular humanism. Hand said very little.

The moderator Arthur Miller—the lawyer, not the play-wright—created a hypothetical community, Sunnyvale, for the panel, and a hypothetical situation: A high-school student named Jennifer brings home an English textbook, an anthology of great American plays including *Dog on a Cold Marble Floor* by the great playwright, Alabama Smith.

The panelists and audience laughed.

Miller turned to Fountain, the hypothetical father, and asked if he wanted his daughter to read this.

"No!" Fountain snapped.

"Why not?" Miller said.

"Because it's tending to subvert the moral stand that I have attempted to teach her at home and I don't feel the school has a right to do this." When Miller appointed a hypothetical teacher, Robert Miller of Miami-Palmetto Senior High School, Fountain took him to task. "You have no right as a school teacher to undermine a set of moral standards—as I said earlier—that I'm seeking to instill in my child, and my point is, that if all of these quote unquote values that we're talking about counteract things that we try to teach in a Judeo-Christian perspective or consensus at home, if it counteracts that, you have no right to teach it to my child."

Robert Miller looked thoughtful. "My response," he said, "is I have not so much a right but a duty to handle the material in a manner that addresses the material not to the student in terms of 'here's a play about adultery, lust, greed, whatever the factor may be, that's the way things ought to be,' but rather 'here's the way this author addressed this subject,' and address it, if I'm an English teacher, as a literary subject. I lament at times the loss of childhood by our students." Fountain nodded. "At the same time I'm conflicted with the feeling that these are senior high students who have a right to know. And you run into that daily as a teacher, the conflict between do you want to protect the remaining innocence of you student or do you wish to exercise, or allow them to exercise, their right to inquire?"

"Okay," Fountain said, "then you're saying that the only way you can learn gracious dining is to eat in a garbage dump."

Audience members looked at each other. Mr. Miller looked confused but he smiled politely. "I'm not sure I follow the logic—"

The audience tittered.

"Okay," Fountain said, "the point that I'm making is that you're saying that a person has to learn about—and we should always point our children toward the higher plane in my opinion, naturally I would—you would expect that of me as a minister. Now the indication that you just gave me is they can only reach that higher plane if they're exposed to all of these things. Now my maintenance is this, that you learn gracious dining by gracious dining."

"But Reverend," protested Nat Hentoff senior editor of The Village Voice, who sat on his left. "You're addressing children in the plural and this started with your daughter, singular. And it seems to me you're saying that by your standards all the children of the school should not be reading this book. How would you feel if the teacher said, 'Look, your position is clear, you don't want your values to be disturbed by this book, your daughter will have an alternative book, but are you saying the book should be banned throughout the school?"

Okay, here's my point," Fountain said. "First of all, we have to consider that as a minister I am functioning not only on the part of my child but ultimately in a case very similar to this I have to ask myself the question, if I am going to not be hypocritical in my ministry, if I am not going to not be hypocritical in my ministry, then if I say to the community that it is wrong for my child to read it, then as a minister in that community, I must assume at the same time, it is wrong for the others to read it."

When Arthur Miller asked if he would let his daughter read an alternative text, Fountain said no. I wondered if this was the root of Pittman's refusal to offer alternative textbooks back in Lake City.

A memory from later that summer: We are driving down to the Gulf, to Keaton Beach, pulling our small sailboat behind us. The boat is named *CORA*, an acronym for Claudia, Ormond, Ross, Anne. We pass a farm with a two-story farmhouse and a long tree-lined drive where a woman and a young child are walking. They are holding hands, wearing boots, swinging buckets, apparently out to pick berries. I feel a pang, sharp desire: *I want to live in the country. I want to walk down a long curving drive with my children to go pick wild berries.*

Jean-Louis Servan-Schreiber once said, in his book about courage, that life is a series of alternations. We had lived in the country outside Bloomington in our one-room cabin overlooking Lake Lemon. When we moved to Lake City, we wanted a big house in town, so we bought the house on Hernando, a wonderful place full of cavernous rooms with high ceilings, twelve-inch pine moldings, and a dining room fit for a board of directors—wainscoting, a built-in china cabinet, a fireplace with a place for the portrait of Ormond's father over the mantle, and a bay window overlooking the pear tree. It was three blocks south of the square, spitting distance from anything we might need for daily life and most rites of passage—church, day-care, grocery store, hospital, florist, or funeral home.

Convenience has its price, we discovered. Our corner was noisy, teens peeling out of the S & S store, trucks grinding their gears at four in the morning. People walked across our front yard, threw trash in our azalea bushes, and parked on our sidewalk. Many times while I was writing, people knocked on the door and asked for odd jobs. A typical trusting middle-class family, we hired all that we could until one itinerant family we'd paid to paint our garage disappeared with most of our tools.

We felt exposed, vulnerable. A few days before we took our sailboat down to the Gulf, I looked out the family room window and saw two boys kicking my car. My first thought was reprisal for the censorship fight. While they smashed a coke bottle over the hood and spit on the windows, I called the police. Two jovial cops made them clean up the mess and then "just to scare them" took them "for a ride" to the Lake City jail. Before they left, I asked the boys why they did it. "Kicks," one boy shrugged. They swore they "ain't never heard of no censorship case."

Even so, we began to go for long drives in the country, slowing down every time we saw "For Sale" on a farmhouse. I wanted to live closer to Tallahassee and Ormond wanted to live close to White Springs, so our rides took us farther north by northwest.

One day in August, we dropped in on Ron and Barb

Ceryak, friends who had built a log home on forty acres in Suwannee County seventeen miles northwest of Lake City. In the midst of an afternoon storm, a real gully washer, we mentioned we wanted a place in the country. Ron and Barb offered to show us some raw land for sale up the road.

We piled in their battered blue pickup and drove through the storm. Ron parked by a pond and said, "This is it."

The four of us sat cramped in the cab. We looked west across a pasture of weeds the color of Nestle's Quick. The windshield wipers flipped rain right and left. We looked north toward a small subtle hill with a wild persimmon tree at the top. Lightning split the dark northern sky. Ormond and I looked at each other.

"We'll take it," we said.

Six.

A small flap with far-reaching effects arose in late August. Board attorney Terry McDavid told Pittman and the board that Sam Jacobson would not file a complaint in U.S. District Court if they placed copies of the banned humanities textbook in the high school library. McDavid was sorely mistaken—Sam had suggested that the textbook committee's recommendation was a reasonable compromise—but faced with what *seemed* like a chance to avoid a costly lawsuit, Little, Haltiwanger, and Chapple voted no. As Chapple put it, "sooner or later they're going to find their way back into the curriculum."

Appropriating the "never give in to terrorists" line of thinking, Keith Hudson said, "If we give in to this threat, we'll be sued by everybody around."

Roger Little agreed. "We've already taken a licking on this from the *Lake City Reporter* in their editorials. I'm not about to back down now, even if it does mean getting sued."

If Little thought he got a licking before, it was nothing compared to what he got the next day. In an editorial on the front page, executive editor Brad Rogers accused Little of sacrificing taxpayers' money "for his own ego gratification." Letters to the editor backed Rogers up, and a second editorial appeared in the paper: "Actually, we understand their position; to have compromised would have meant softening a completely stupid action to one that was only ignorant. Better to be consistent."

The "Columbia Consensus" reflected a slight shift in local sentiment when a record number of callers answered the question:

> Do you agree with the school board's rejection of a compromise in the book ban issue?
> YES 61% NO 39%
> (101 responses)

> Yes, the books should not be put in the hands of young children. Yes, I don't want my children reading that trash in the schools. Yes, this type of literature should be removed from the schools. Yes, I'm a student at CHS and I don't think we should have to read pornography at school. Yes, they shouldn't even listen to those people. No, as a senior at CHS, I think they've violated my rights. They've proven how ignorant they are. No, I have been appalled by the position taken by Pittman and the school board. No, it certainly shows how ridiculous our elected officials can be to allow a few religious nuts to make the decisions for the county. They're going to find out in the next election they were wrong ...

The percentage of people who agreed with the school board was down thirteen percent. Pittman put the matter on the agenda for the September 8 meeting.

As September approached, I made a nostalgic note in my journal about the summer I'd spent home with the children:

> They are blond heads, soft straight hair, brilliant babies now grown husky—Ross, almost five, and Anne, almost nine, sitting in my lap last week, the two of us talking away. I said to her you are like, no, this is like having a baby again but one who can carry on a brilliant conversation.

In late August Anne started fourth grade, and Ross began kindergarten. Ormond and I worried that he might be too young—his is a late August birthday—but he seemed happy to go. I was glad to get back to the novel.

After a summer away from my work, reentry has always been hard. I know I'm ready to write when I have this dream in late August: a snarling beast appears and terrifies me until I realize that it's my ambition. Name it and you will have power over it, folk wisdom says. When I recognize the beast in my dream, he is calmed, ambition integrated into my life once again.

I was aware, as I returned to Roz's life in Ohumpka, how my life in Lake City—especially the censorship fight—was informing the story as I went along. When I'd set it aside at the start of the summer, Roz had just attended her first story meeting up in Atlanta. Now, returning home to write scripts for *Heart's Curtain*, she needed some kind of day care for her four-year-old, Jon. The only preschool in Ohumpka was Our Father's Children, run by a fundamentalist preacher named Reverend Reymond.

I began chapter four. Roz swallows her secular humanist pride, and enrolls Jon in the preschool. Both are happy until Reymond calls her into his office, enraged that she let her son bring *The Tale of Two Bad Mice* to school. The story, in the preacher's opinion, promotes breaking and entering, vandalism, and theft.

I laughed as I worked on this scene, a satire of the Lake City case, the far-fetched accusations Fritz Fountain had made. A few days later, I read about a censorship case bound for U.S. District Court in Tennessee: fundamentalists were suing their school board for exposing their children to material that violated their religious beliefs. They cited more than four hundred objectionable sections from books including *The Diary of Anne Frank* (because it suggested all religions were equal), and *The Wizard of Oz* (because it had a good witch and depicted traits such as courage, intelligence and compassion as personally developed rather than God-given).

I copied this into my journal and added a note, "This makes my scene with Reverend Reymond too real to be funny," then I returned to the scene and made an addition: Roz defends the two mice. They repent, she points out: Hunca Munca sweeps up and Tom Thumb pays for the damage with a sixpence he finds under the hearth rug. Even worse, the Reverend roars: their repentance was personally developed; it wasn't God-given.

On September 8, a real scorcher, I called Sam Jacobson. I wanted to know if I could stay on the censorship case when Ormond and I built a house on our land and moved out of the county. He said I could. I found it hard to believe that the case would still be in the courts by the time we sold our house on Hernando and finished the cracker farmhouse we wanted to build, but Jim Virgil kept saying, "This one's going all the way."

Ormond and I drove to a real estate agency out by the mall and listed our house. The realtor—a smooth-talking man with straight soft gray hair—set the price lower than we would have liked but he said the house would sell faster this way. We agreed. The sooner we sold the house, the sooner we could start building.

That night, the school board met and reconsidered its decision to keep *Lysistrata* and "The Miller's Tale" out of the library at Columbia High. McDavid, having since been corrected by Jacobson, "ate crow," as he put it, and said he was "only throwing out suggestions and/or possibilities that occurred to him during a conversation with Sam Jacobson. It was just 'lawyer talk.'" He apologized to the board for causing the misunderstanding and clarified our position that the only acceptable compromise was the textbook committee's recommendation.

Pittman said he got "The Miller's Tale" and *Lysistrata* out and read them again, but this time he could find "no redeeming qualities *whatsoever*." In addition to his previous complaints about *Lysistrata*, he was now offended by the translator's use of Southern dialect to depict characters from Sparta. "I don't want it in the classroom," he said, but he reluctantly agreed to put it in the library on a "mature reading shelf."

Dianne Lane turned to Pittman. "If we put it in the library, why not accept the textbook committee's report?"

"I opposed it and I still oppose it," Pittman snapped. "This is not my idea of Chaucer's *Canterbury Tales*." He insisted that "The Miller's Tale" he'd read in school had been in Old English.

He told Lane he was "appalled" that she would consider placing the books in the classroom after she'd read them. Lane sighed and proposed placing a copy in the library. Little relented. So did Haltiwanger and Hudson. Only Chapple opposed. The motion carried four to one.

The next morning I told Sam Jacobson what the board had decided. He said he would prepare a formal complaint to be filed sometime in the fall with the U.S. District Court. Susan called the high school librarian who told her that copies of "The Miller's Tale" and *Lysistrata* had been part of the library's collection for years. Apparently it hadn't occurred to the school board to see if they were already there.

In late September we closed the deal on the land. Ormond and I drove the seventeen miles from Lake City to Live Oak, the small town that would be our new home. I had some misgivings about moving there—it was half the size of Lake City—but it loved football better than Jesus and so far its school board hadn't banned books. It didn't seem half as smug or self-righteous; it knew what it was and it made jokes about it: T-shirts said WELCOME TO LIVE OAK, AN ELEVEN BULLDOG ONE HORSE TOWN. And there is something downright Chaucerian about a place where two of the prominent families are named Cheeks and Crapps.

We signed the papers and drove to our land. Ormond took his machete and made a small clearing down by the pond for our picnic table. We sat and contemplated our future home, our acres of weeds—goldenrod, dotted horsemen, fleabane, loco weed. We're we crazy? Thirty-two acres of weeds? But we could see it, oh, we could see it: a cracker farmhouse with exposed rafter tails and wide porches—overlooking a meadow we'd plant in bahia—surrounded by twenty acres of pines.

Meadowfront property.

It seemed like the best of both worlds, "the broad ease of the farmland," as Virgil says in *The Georgics*, in the midst of an enclave of back-to-the-landers—most of them geologists like Ron Ceryak—and the Baileys, farmers who homesteaded the region.

For the rest of September and on into October, we went to the land every weekend. The work was hard but ecstatic. We cleared brush and tyty down by the pond. Once, amid blackgums—a tree that looks like a cypress but does not produce knees—Ormond cut a section of tyty and lifted it over his head, unaware that a water moccasin was dangling down from the branch. I said, "Sn—Sn—Sn—," but I couldn't get the word out. Finally I did. He hurled the snake in the pond.

We burned piles of brush. We built a shed northeast of the site for the used tractor we'd bought, then we planted our meadow in the late summer heat: Ormond slowly disking the ground with the tractor as I walked behind cranking bahia seed out of a canvas seed-caster—agriculture's organ grinder.

We staked our future homesite. We marked the sections of land where pines would be planted after the new year and we discovered that the hill just north of our home site was covered with wild blackberry bushes. Ross, barely five, named the farm Blackberry Hill.

In early October, in Alabama, Judge W. Brevard Hand presided over the two-and-a-half-week-long trial of the forty-five textbooks. On October 25, I read a headline about the case in Tennessee: PARENTS WIN COURT RULING ON TEXT-BOOKS. U.S. District Judge Thomas G. Hull had ruled that students could not be forcibly exposed to material that violated their religious beliefs. I scanned the list of books banned, not only *Diary of Anne Frank* and *The Wizard of Oz* but also *Cinderella*, *Macbeth*, writings by Isaac Asimov, Hans Christian Andersen, Margaret Mead, and "The Revolt of Mother," a seventh-grade short story about a woman challenging her husband's authority and therefore challenging the "biblical family." All, according to Hull, were "stimulation of children's imaginations beyond the limitations of scriptural authority." The school board appealed Hull's decision.

Our case was dubbed "a turnabout of the Tennessee case" by the *Florida Times Union* on November 25:

> Required reading of some literary classics in a rural Tennessee school district was found by a federal judge last month to have violated the religious freedom of some fundamentalist Christians.
>
> A turnabout of that case was launched yesterday in U.S. District Court in Jacksonville by a group of parents who charged that their religious freedom was violated when the Columbia

County School Board banned a textbook that included adaptations of two classic stories that were not required reading for students.

I was serving iced tea to Silas Pittman at Ross's Thanksgiving Day dinner at the Kindergarten Center when Jacobson filed a complaint with the U.S. District Court, Middle District of Florida, Jacksonville Division.

After setting down the facts of the case, the complaint simply stated that we sought to enjoin the banning of the textbook which constituted a suppression of speech and thought and an abridgment of freedom of speech:

> The action of defendants further constitutes an establishment of religion and a prohibition upon the freedom thereof, and a violation of the principle of separation of church and state inherent in constitutional freedom of religion. The actions of defendants accordingly are violative of rights secured by the First and Fourteenth Amendments to the Constitution of the United States.
>
> WHEREFORE plaintiffs seek the following relief:
>
> 1. A declaration that the action and conduct of defendants is violative of the First and Fourteenth Amendments to the Constitution of the United States.
>
> 2. A temporary and thereafter permanent injunction restraining and enjoining defendants from suppression of *Humanities*.
>
> 3. An order requiring defendants to pay and be responsible for reasonable fees and costs incident to this action.
>
> 4. An order providing such further relief as to the Court seems appropriate.

When news of the complaint hit the papers, National Public Radio picked up the story. Pittman stuck to his position but surpassed his previous syntax. "I don't feel that expressions that students make in the hall they'd be suspended for should be put in the classroom. If I were embarrassed to read passages from either one of these two selections in front of the School Board, if I were embarrassed to do that and I would be, then that is my more or less, you know, determining factor as to what we should do and what we shouldn't do."

Chairman Chapple concurred. "If the school board can't censor them, who can? That's my thoughts on that. Somebody needs to censor them. I just think it was a little—excuse the expression—'trashy' for students."

NPR reported with great amusement that humanities students, shorn of their textbooks back in April, were left to watch movies in class, films such as *Jaws* and *Ghostbusters*, the latter replete with the "f" word. This elicited more ridicule including a letter in the *St. Petersburg Times*:

> The state-approved textbook was taken from the students and locked up. One school board member declared the excerpts in question as "trashy."
>
> Aristophanes and Chaucer, trashy?
>
> The students, deprived of their textbooks, viewed rented tapes of *Ghostbusters* and *Jaws* during class. Perhaps the Columbia County School Board considers the writhings of Sigourney Weaver and a mechanical fish part of the great content of Western civilization.

Mary Ann Witt—controlling editor of the banned textbook—was not amused when she happened to hear the story on NPR at her home in North Carolina. It was the first time her book had ever been banned. Shocked by the news, she contacted Sharon Saunders at the *Lake City Reporter*. "The idea of censorship, bowing to the wishes of a few people, is very frightening and objectionable," she said. "I understand that it might not be appropriate to assign the two selections, but I do not understand the banning of the entire book. I can't believe the board could be so easily swayed by a small minority."

The local reaction to our complaint was purely economic: people were concerned about the cost of a lawsuit, especially when the board hired the Jacksonville law firm of Coker, Myers

& Schickel which was happy to handle the case; as Vonnegut says in "Palm Sunday": "There is never a shortage anywhere of lawyers eager to attack the First Amendment, as though it were nothing more than a clause in a lease from a crooked slumlord."

In mid-December the school board reassured the taxpayers that the censorship case would not cost them a penny. The board had a self-insurance plan with the Northeast Florida Educational Consortium. Jim Virgil, silent since his speech to the school board on May 27, responded in a letter to the editor:

> When the book suit is over, the legal bills will be horrific. When the insurance company pays for them, what do you think will happen to the annual rate they will charge for next year's premium? I'm sorry to inform The Reporter that there is no Tooth Fairy, no Easter Bunny and no such thing as 'no cost' insured loss.

The cost of joining the consortium was $370,000.

Seven.

1987 began happily with a letter from the novelist, David Brin.

Susan had written to him when she noticed he'd dedicated his novel *The Postman* to Lysistrata. On January 1, he answered her letter:

> Dear Susan Davis,
> It was distressing to hear about your problems with the Lake City School Board's decison to remove anything even vaguely controversial from the English curriculum. (I don't imagine they'd allow *The Postman* into the school libraries, although the American Library Association called it one of the "best for young adults," sigh.) Of course we are living in a time of conflict. New myths are being forged and old tribal systems fading. This frightens some, who believe that only in stable, rigid reverence of former ways will there be any possible salvation.
> Did you know that, in the 1920's, it was widely bruited that the *saxophone* was "the devil's flute," and that *any* decent young girl who heard a few bars of its crooning, seductive tones would be inexorably drawn into a frenzy of uncontrollable sexual passion? I tell you of this example because it elucidates what I believe lies at the heart of this debate. It is not morality or freedom, but a difference of opinion about the fundamental strengths of young human

beings.

There are those who believe that people are fundamentally strong. That, given an open access to all knowledge, along with loving guidance by teachers and parents, students will learn about the dangers of the world and make correct decisions as a result. I have seen this work in practice. There are also those, however, who believe that young people are frail, delicate, and easily enticed into evil ways. Of course they are right ... I've seen it happen lots of times. Cults, drugs, sado-masochistic sexuality, all of these call seductively, as does simplistic religion. But when these people try to defend their children by erecting high walls of simplistic morality, protecting them from all the enticements outside, they actually *weaken* their offspring terribly.

The statistics are plain. Where there is sex education (accompanied, perhaps, by close parental involvement) there is not only lower teenage pregnancy incidence, but also lower rates of premarital sexual activity! With the mystery removed, the girls become much more ferocious in their self protection.

At the heart of a solution will be to show these parents the truth. That we progressives are not all instruments of the devil. That, in the end, we also would rather see our children have white weddings and happy families than become warped psychopaths, that our argument is more over *means* than ends, and that we believe *knowledge* is a better tool than ignorance.

If there is any way I can help in your local battle against darkness, please let me know.

Sincerely, David Brin

Susan gave the letter to Monya who, per our division of labor, made us all copies. I carried mine around for a couple of days—a pep talk in my purse—then added it to the burgeoning pile of documentation.

Brin confirmed my belief that our case, perhaps any

censorship case, was inherently comic, albeit a comedy of terrors. His phrase "stable, rigid reverence" brought Fountain, Pittman, and the school board to mind but also Henri Bergson's essay on laughter: A major element of comedy, he says, is "inelasticity." Censors like Pittman and Fountain, in their extremism, suffer from what Bergson calls "a curvature of the soul."

More important, Brin's letter broadened the boundaries of our battle and deepened the implications of censorship, at least in the schools. At first glance, the issue for the school board was morality; for us it was intellectual freedom. But Brin was right—there was something much deeper at stake. We were suing for our children's right to receive information because ignorance was the absence of knowledge and knowledge was power. The issue for us was empowering children.

A few days after Brin's letter arrived, a *St. Petersburg Times* reporter named Larry King drove up to Lake City to write about our censorship case. He talked to the school board and Silas Pittman and a number of other people in town, though not to Fritz Fountain, who had started stonewalling the press.

He met with Jim, Monya, Susan, and me at the Virgil's ranch house, which backed on a pasture of cattle just north of town.

He asked us to characterize Lake City, Florida. Now, six years later, after dealing with reporters dozens and dozens of times, I would be wary of a question like that. I would sniff out its purpose—hot copy. I would know what one reporter has told me—I'm what they call "dial-a-quote." But all I could see when King asked the question was a chance to get even with a town that had censored my two favorite classics, a chance to say how absurd it all was. And I figured I could say what I pleased (didn't I always?) because you couldn't buy the *St. Petersburg Times* in Lake City.

My momma told me my mouth would get me in trouble.

"How would I characterize Lake City, Florida?" I leaned back in my chair. King leaned forward, pen poised over paper. "I would characterize Lake City as devoted to mediocrity, a daily study in stupidity, but it ceases to be funny when you run into a case of censorship."

I told him my forehead was beginning to slant backward, I'd slapped it so often in disbelief. The four of us regaled him with our favorite Lake City stories: the sheriff who held a public burning of bales of marijuana that were, it turned out, garden mulch; the dozens of people who responded to a Chamber of Commerce invitation with the question, "What does R.S.V.P. mean?"; the man who had an attack of Lake City machismo and tried to bite the head off a live rattlesnake only to be bitten badly himself.

"Not to mention banning of a state-approved humanities textbook," Jim added. "Here's a bunch of damn provincial politicians depriving our kids of classics. It's ridiculous. It offends me. What do they take out next? Where do they stop? They don't do on Monday nights and Saturday nights what they do on Sunday mornings, let's put it that way. It's a very hypocritical society."

King left, absolutely delighted. He promised to send us a copy of Sunday's *St. Petersburg Times*.

Around noon on Monday, Sharon Saunders called from the *Lake City Reporter* to tell me my remarks had enraged most of the staff.

I asked, "What remarks?"

"The ones on the front page of the *Lake City Reporter*."

I asked her to wait while I stepped outside to pick up my copy and see what I'd said. The article liberally quoted what King had written the day before in the *St. Petersburg Times*. King had characterized us as "three Reaganite Republicans and a liberal, Berkeley-educated feminist named Claudia Johnson. She is no diplomat." My remarks, and Jim Virgil's, were quoted in full.

I returned to the phone. "Sharon," I said, "just one question. How did you get these remarks? Did Larry King tell you?"

"No," she said, "his story went on the A.P. wire."

"Ah."

"The staff here at the paper thinks you ought to retract your remarks."

"Oh?" I said drily. "What happened to freedom of speech?"

"Then you don't want to change them?"

"Actually, Sharon, I think I was kind."

She laughed and agreed. Her husband, also black, had already fled to Tallahassee; they were living apart because, in his opinion, Lake City was "an uninhabitable place." She planned to join him when she could find work.

I was roundly attacked for my remarks. One letter to the editor threatened to sue me for libel. Another accused the A.C.L.U. of being "the criminals' lobby" and concluded: "Miss Johnson, if Lake City is 'devoted to mediocrity, a daily study in stupidity,' may I remind you 'Delta is ready when you are!'"

I was baffled by this reference to Delta. What did the fourth letter of the Greek alphabet or a deposit of sand at the mouth of a river have to do with me or my remarks?

"Delta, Delta," I muttered to Ormond.

"The airline," he said.

Jim fared much worse. As the newly elected president of the Chamber of Commerce, he was attacked by the school board on January 13 for casting Lake City in a negative light.

"This offends me," said Keith Hudson. "I thought the chamber was supposed to promote Columbia County."

Roger Little agreed, "To me he is demoting Lake City." Board attorney McDavid accused Virgil of being "no booster of the school board. This type of leadership is a detriment to the community. As long as people in leadership positions are not promoting Lake City and are critical, Lake City is not going to progress."

The board drafted a letter stating that Virgil's remarks were "derogatory and unfounded."

Jim responded that he had spoken as a private citizen, not as the president of the Chamber of Commerce.

> The fact that the rest of the state now ridicules us is a result of your actions, not mine. Your record of negative images is consistent. You have lost a race discrimination lawsuit to the N.A.A.C.P. You now have a censorship lawsuit being waged against you. On top of all this you cannot seem to fix the roof at the high school which has been leaking every time it rains the past six to eight years.

The Chamber backed him up:

> Jim Virgil's personal views and preferences are exactly that and should in no way be construed as being that of the Chamber of Commerce. We are fortunate to live in a country that allows freedom of speech and the Chamber of Commerce recognizes the right of every individual to freely express his or her opinion.

The school board finally backed down. Roger Little glumly conceded that Jim was expressing a personal view.

"He's entitled to that even if it is negative. I say negative things, too, sometimes," Little said.

The face of Suwannee County was changing. Bounded on the north, west, and south by the meandering Suwannee and to the east by Lake City's Columbia County, it is a county defined by its farming.

"It used to be that a person driving around the county in the summertime would see fields of corn, soybeans, peanuts and tobacco," wrote farm editor Thornton Hartley. "Someone who has not seen those fields lately may be surprised to find that many of them are green with young pines instead of corn or soybeans." The thirty-two acres we bought had once been rich farmland but they had been fallow for years, gone to brittle brown weeds. Ormond and I had no intention of farming; we could barely grow a tomato. So, like many others around us, we planted pines.

On January 17, a cold drizzly day, the Forestry Service delivered the trees we had ordered—sixteen thousand improved slash pines, *Pinus ellioti*—which arrived, to our surprise, in several small bundles. We hired Gary Locke, a planter from Wellborn, who drove the lead tractor and "scalped" the land into furrows while two tractors followed with platforms in tow for the "setters"—men hunched over in bright yellow slickers who planted a pine tree every four feet. The whole operation took less than four hours.

Afterward, Ormond and I stood in the drizzle and marveled at what had been raw land, all weeds, a few months before. Now it was a field of bahia surrounded by small scraggy pines a hand high. Locke told us we'd have privacy in a couple of years—improved slash pines grew three feet a year. We could harvest in twenty years, maybe sooner, our land was so fertile. This was why we'd planted the trees, to raise money for Anne and Ross's college tuition, or, if we didn't harvest in time, to pay ourselves back for the land.

We weren't alone in making financial plans for the future. Two weeks before, out in Tulsa, Oral Roberts had announced that he must raise 4.5 million dollars or he was going to die. Back in 1980 he'd had a vision of a 900-foot Jesus standing over his City of Faith Medical Center. After the vision, followers contributed five million dollars for the three-tower, sixty-story complex. In March 1986 God told Roberts he had until the end of the year to raise the remaining amount that he needed, but as the year had come to an end, God cut him some slack. The new deadline, God told him, was March 31.

Our own plans to build moved along. A week later we got an offer on our house on Hernando. The couple who wanted to buy it were Jehovah's Witnesses moving into Lake City. I had mixed emotions about helping more zealots move into town, but we had no other offers so, like Oral Roberts, we agreed to a late March closing date.

In early February, an editorial appeared in the *Miami Herald*:

> If you were asked to name a category in which Florida's schools lead the nation, what would you guess? Test scores? No. Teacher pay? Not even close. College research? Fat chance! Yet there is such a category: censorship. According to a survey by People for the American Way, Florida's public schools reported seven incidents of official censorship last year. No other state has as many. The worst brouhaha was in the North Florida town of Lake City ...

After outlining our case, the editorial insisted that elected officials must "entrust book selection to the professional judgment of teachers and librarians. Any who egregiously abuse that trust may be held accountable—just as school board members who resort to censorship should be held accountable."

On February 12, John J. Shickel accounted for the school board's actions in his "Answers to Standard Interrogatories." He listed as affirmative defenses:

> 1) The School Board has absolute discretion in the matters of curriculum.
>
> 2) We deny that the School Board was motivated for religious, political or any ulterior motives and affirmatively state that the motives for removing the adaptations of the pieces was in the best interest of the students and the educational process.
>
> 3) The School Board continues to remit the originals of the works referred to be in the library of the various schools involved and that it was only this particular adaptation that was removed from the curriculum.

Eight days later the Florida Department of Education approved the banned textbook again for use in the state. The *Lake City Reporter* responded with an editorial blasting the school board for being the only one out of Florida's sixty-six counties to deny students access to the book:

> Our nearly-adult children's morals were declared safe from the terrible language (in "The Miller's Tale") and ideas (women's lib in "Lysistrata") that might bring their minds into the 20th century and put them on an equal level with high school students elsewhere in the Sunshine State.

State-approved status provided no protection against censorship in Alabama, either. On March 4, while Oral Roberts' son, Richard, begged viewers to "sow a seed on your Visa, your MasterCard," Judge Hand sowed one for the censors, ruling that secular humanism was a religion; *ergo,* the use of the forty-five challenged textbooks violated the U.S. Constitution's prohibition against government establishment of religion. Thirty social studies, nine history, and six home economics textbooks were purged from school shelves, "a frightening censorship aimed at giving religious fundamentalists a foot in the schoolhouse door," one critic called it.

Hand, of course, denied it was censorship. "This case is not an attempt by anyone to censor materials deemed undesirable, improper or immoral. What this case is about is the allegedly improper promotion of certain religious beliefs." Appeal motions were filed with the 11th U.S. Circuit Court of Appeals the following week.

With our house on Hernando about to change hands, I scouted rentals in town and found a house we could live in while we built our house at the farm. The house was small, dank, and gray—a mouse of a house—with a shocking pink master bedroom that Susan and Monya helped me paint white. Ormond and I nicknamed it "Mildew Haven" and planned to move in before closing.

We found a young architect, Chip Sawyer, who studied the lay of the land, the site we had chosen, and our pencil sketches. We wanted a great room and loft—a reprise of our cabin in Indiana—a screened porch for a hammock off the master bedroom, and a big L-shaped porch overlooking the meadow and pond. Chip took it from there and began what he called "the design phase."

I won the Maud Adams playwriting award for my full-length play, *Y.* The prize, awarded by Stephens College, included a main-stage production and a round-trip air ticket. The date of the show was already set—the same week we were closing. Ormond said he could manage; I could sign all the papers and we could move the big stuff to Mildew Haven before I left for Missouri. He would sweat the small stuff while I was away.

Meanwhile, I worked on my dissertation. I planned to finish a first draft by June, but it still wasn't titled. I'd tossed out *Heart's Curtain*—too downbeat for this romp of a novel—but I hadn't come up with anything better. I agonized; I was in what

Jerry Stern called "title hell." What was the right title for a novel about soap opera, fundamentalists, and pornography? One day I found it right in the text—*Organ Music*.

On top of all this good news, Indiana—the place where Ormond and I met, married, had our first baby, and bought our first house—had a wonderful basketball team; they just might win a national title if they could knock off U.N.L.V.

In mid-March, two weeks before I left for Missouri, the realtor called and said the buyers wanted to close a week early to lock in low interest rates. Ormond and I talked it over; we knew we couldn't move out any faster, but we would close early if it didn't affect the date of possession. The realtor assured us it wouldn't.

The next two weeks went by in a boxes-and-packing-tape blur. While we packed, someone donated 1.3 million dollars and saved Oral Roberts. Jimmy Swaggart accused Jim Bakker of a one-night stand with a former secretary six years before. Bakker said he had long since repented and Swaggart wanted control of the Praise The Lord Club. Jessica Hahn came forward and said she was the woman; her lawyer said Bakker had lured, drugged, and seduced her, then bought her silence for $265,000. Wags called it "Pearlygate."

As we had promised, Ormond and I closed a week early. The closing went smoothly until money changed hands and the new owners demanded a key to the house. The realtor reminded them that the date of possession was not for a week. We nodded. The new owners didn't. The meek blonde-haired Jehovah's Witness wife rose out of her chair and shrieked at the realtor, "*You mean we just gave them our money and we can't get a key?*" She and her husband stormed out, slamming the door.

The realtor turned his doe-eyes on me. "Help me out here," he pleaded. "They do have a point. They just gave you their money. The least we could do is give them a key."

We sat there a moment. There were fragile, irreplaceable things in our house on Hernando. His late parents' china and crystal. His father's portrait. Folk artifacts. Ormond had a look on his face that said what my character Tom would say a week later in *Y*, "Hey, I'm a nice person. I don't kick dogs." Finally, against his best instincts, he told the realtor to give them a key.

I flew to Missouri. *Y* was a hit. Indiana beat U.N.L.V. And the new owners let themselves in and promptly changed the locks on the house.

Ormond called *in extremis*. He couldn't get in. He couldn't get his late parents' china or crystal or his dad's portrait out. He couldn't get in touch with the owners. The realtor wasn't returning his calls. Our friends the Richards and Kings came to the rescue, taking care of the kids so Ormond could camp outside the house until the new owners appeared. When they did, they grudgingly opened the door. He got our stuff out.

I returned from Missouri, we moved into Mildew Haven, and Indiana won the national title. But the stress had taken its toll. We were exhausted. There was little but tension between us, except perhaps resentment and blame. I blamed Lake City and the year-long ordeal of the censorship case, which Ormond took to mean I blamed him for moving me there. He blamed the realtor and the couple who bought the house on Hernando, which I took to mean he blamed me for violating two of the rules that we lived by: Never put your trust in a realtor and never *ever* let a Jehovah's Witness into your house.

A few days after we moved into Mildew Haven, the telephone rang. I answered. It was Bobby Abernathy, a musician who played the piano at a bar in Lake City. His mother owned the other half of our pond in Suwannee County. He was calling to tell us he'd hired a surveyor—the same man who had surveyed our land—to survey his mother's farm. In the process, he had discovered he'd "made a mistake fourteen years before"—the corner marker down by our gate was a few inches off. This meant, Abernathy informed me, that we no longer owned the drive into our land. It belonged to his mother. So did almost all of the pond.

Stunned, I put down the phone. Ormond and I took the children and drove up to the land. Abernathy had already strung a new fence across the old road. We couldn't drive in.

I tried to get a second opinion but ran into the "old buddy system" all over again: No surveyor would go against the man who said he made a mistake. I appealed to Mike Harrell who sold us our title insurance, but he called it "an honest mistake."

Looking back, I know we should have hired a lawyer but I also know why we didn't. I couldn't face a second lawsuit; a person can only fight so many battles. Instead we rented a box scraper and cut a new road through our pines.

In the next few weeks, Abernathy extended the fence along the new property line, denying us access to most of the pond. The Department of Environmental Regulation said this was strictly illegal but would not take the case. We were welcome to sue. Something snapped. I couldn't do it. I couldn't live in rural North Florida. I couldn't live where I didn't feel welcome. When I said so to Ormond, he told me that he couldn't leave. He had an excellent job; where would he, a *folklorist*, find another? And I had no job at all except for a teaching assistant-ship at Florida State in the fall, hardly enough to support us.

Couldn't leave, couldn't stay.

One day in late April Chip Sawyer called. The house plan was finished. Ormond and I drove down to his office in Gainesville. Chip unrolled the blueprint. There it was, the home that we'd hoped for, a real cracker gem. I sat there torn between wanting to build this beautiful house and knowing that I couldn't live there.

On April 27, I made five quick notes in my journal:

1. Ross wanted to take dog tags this morning for his "share day." I said fine. He said: Do you know why soldiers had dog tags?

No, I said.

Well, he said, they didn't have much fun fighting the war so the dog tag has their birthday on it so their friends can know when it is."

2. Gunman on spree, killed 6 in S. Florida. Won't affect two bills before the state house to ease gun control legislation. As congressman Wayne Hollingsworth said: If some private citizen had had his gun with him, he might could have shot him. Wayne Hollingsworth is from Lake City.

3. Jim Bakker now accused of homosexuality and using prostitutes. Assemblies of God said they

can restore a fallen minister for alcoholism, family problems, using prostitutes, but never for homosexuality.

4. 5 1/2 weeks to finish the novel.

5. Going to see Pat Korb on Friday.

Back when I wrote for *The Catlins*, Pat had helped me regain my sense of humor. Now, my marriage at stake, I wanted to see her again:

> Much internal & external shrieking about committing to the house—but feeling now the compromise may be: build the farmhouse for Ormond but the kids and I will live, go to school, in Tally during the week—have the farmhouse we want as a weekend retreat.
>
> Totally eccentric plan; just may work.

The truth was, I loved Tallahassee. I had found there what Matthew Arnold described as "a current of ideas ... animating and nourishing to the creative power," what Tennessee Williams called "high octane." Ormond knew this; he'd nicknamed it "Tallahappiness." The solution seemed simple to me—well, hardly simple—fragmented, expensive—but when I mentioned the two-household option to him, he walked out of the room.

Two days later I wrote:

> O. so grim, sad, angry at the suggestion of our move to Tallahassee—I've been angry, depressed, with a headache for weeks now. Once, in the middle of the night, I began crying—panicked that I was losing my grip on mental health and knowing I couldn't, that I had to be there for the kids. Woke O. & cried & raved & blamed him—slept it off—but that is terror, feeling yourself cracking up.
>
> What I don't know & may never know is whether O. would stay depressed or adjust to the situation—I've never adjusted to Lake City—if I believed he would I would go in a minute ...

It's exhausting not knowing.
And will I ever?
About anything?

Eight.

I saw Pat Korb on the first of May. That it was May Day was not lost on me.

I told her about waking up in cold sweats, terrified about cracking up and not being there for my children. I told her about the censorship fight, buying the land, planting pines, losing the road and the pond, my ambivalence about building the house and being able to live there.

She said, "You feel as though you are mortgaging yourself."

"Yes." I exhaled. It was like a benediction; someone understood how I felt.

She said each of us is territorial. We must—a necessity, not a luxury—live in a place where we feel at home. And each of us has an inner core that is inviolate. Mine had been violated when the board banned two classics I loved and again when we were fenced off our land.

She passed the Kleenex. "You have burnout," she said. "Do you recognize it?" I didn't. I suspected I might with my writing (I often do by the time summer comes) but she said no, it was with anger, with fighting the place where I lived, the bad fit. I was right when I told Ormond I could not fight more battles, at least for the moment. I was burned out.

I told her I couldn't decide what to do.

Pat leaned forward. "Of course you can't. As long as you want your family, and I think you do, you have to make the decision with Ormond. The old models don't work. You and Ormond must build your own."

Ormond went to see Pat the next day. I knew he was scared. I was scared, too. What if he decided to decide by himself? What would be his decision?

Fainthearted, I read Rollo May's *The Courage to Create* until Ormond came home. May's words on this, the second of May, seemed downright uncanny, and I copied them into my journal:

> A choice confronts us. Shall we, as we feel our foundations shaking, withdraw in anxiety and panic? Frightened by the loss of our familiar mooring places, shall we become paralyzed and cover our inaction with apathy? If we do those things, we will have surrendered our chance to participate in the forming of the future ... if you do not express your own original ideas, if you do not listen to your own being, you will have betrayed yourself.

I heard Ormond pull into the driveway. I opened the door. He got out of the car, my lanky long-suffering husband, and told me he loved me. I took this to mean we'd be deciding together.

That afternoon we drove up to the land and sat on the hill. Anne and Ross roasted marshmallows down by the shed while Ormond and I watched a real rah-rah sunset, garish school colors, purple and gold. The breeze was brisk, from the south, from the pond with its raucous chorus of frogs.

Ormond described his session with Pat. She'd asked him to list his needs. Colleagues, like-minded people, feeling at home in the place where he lived, were not on his list; they had been on mine. He'd realized he probably needed these more than he thought, and I clearly did. He didn't say we would try the two-household family, but the possibility seemed to be in the air.

We made an appointment to see Pat Korb together. Her only free time was Sunday, Mother's Day, May 10. By the time it arrived, we were angry again.

A few days before, we'd gone to the Kindergarten Center to see Ross in the end-of-the-year extravaganza about the four seasons. Ross was "April," a white bunny with pink overstuffed ears. Later, at lunch, I told Ormond I thought Ross was too young to go on to first grade. The youngest child in his class, his self esteem seemed to be sliding. He was getting picked on at the playground. He came home exhausted. Tallahasee offered a primer year designed for students like Ross—bright but too young for first grade.

Ormond guessed rightly where this was leading: Anne would have better schools, and I would be living where I felt at home. Terrified of losing his family, he said he didn't want us to move.

"Then quit your job and go with us."

He lashed out. If he *lost* his job he wouldn't move to Tallahassee. He would stay in Suwannee County no matter what.

"Well, *fuck him!*" I wrote that night in my journal. "Much as I love him & the houseplan it is evident (& somewhat depressing) that I will have to churchkey the kids and me out."

We were hardly speaking by Mother's Day morning. I feigned cheer as Anne and Ross brought me breakfast in bed—bagels, orange juice, bean-ground coffee—and cards and gifts—a silk flower in a cardboard vase Ross had made and two hearts he'd embroidered on burlap; a barrette Anne had covered with rainbow paper and hearts. The sitter arrived. Ormond and I drove in silence to Gainesville.

Pat Korb asked us to state our resentments.

Ormond went first. He said I didn't appreciate how hard all this was for him, how hard he was trying.

I resented his having it all under one umbrella.

He resented my resentment. It was *our* umbrella based on numerous decisions we'd made together.

I snarled, "I didn't decide to ban books."

Pat Korb was so astonished she laughed. "I've never seen a couple so polarized. You won't let each other finish a *sentence*."

We worked on listening skills.

He spoke. I tried to listen, then I stated what I thought he'd said.

No, he told me, that wasn't it.

We started over again.

When it was my turn, I spoke. He tried to listen. He repeated what he thought I'd said.

No, I told him. No, no, no, no, *no*.

We slogged on, exhausted, we, the hearing impaired.

You said. I need. We decided.

After an hour, Pat thought we'd made progress. I was too tired to tell. She suggested that we sell the land and look for a place halfway between Tallahasee and Live Oak. That meant Madison, Monticello. We told her we already had. The schools worried me, we couldn't find land that we liked, and the last thing I wanted was to break in another small town in north Florida. I wanted to live in a town that I liked, the town where I worked.

Pat turned to Ormond, "You have to let Claudia experience her professional self."

Ormond nodded, but the set of his jaw said that he felt bitter, betrayed. I felt guilty.

He took the hurt, the hard jaw, to work Monday morning. Ross took it to heart and threw up. I took Anne to school and put Ross back to bed and then I called Ormond. I said I was sorry.

"It's too late," he said.

I put down the phone. When all this started, he was worried about burning crosses. Now it looked like our marriage had gone up in smoke.

Ross woke up before lunch. His stomach felt better. Mine felt worse but I didn't let on. I asked if he'd like to pack up a picnic and drive to the land. He brightened. I called Ormond's office and left a message that he was welcome to join us. I knew he would not.

Ross and I drove to the farm. We spread our food on the table down by the pond. Ross ate his sandwich. The fresh air and sunshine did us both good. He asked if he could walk down the driveway and visit a neighbor, Nicole. I said he could.

I sat alone and stared at the pond, at the blackgums, the tyty, Abernathy's barbed-wire fence. It was warm, but the breeze off the water was cool. Wild violets, purple and white, dotted the spongy ground by the pond.

I turned and looked out at the land, at the bahia we'd

planted the previous fall. I got down from the table and walked into the meadow, patchy with whorls of bahia. I'd asked Pat Korb what I should do when I got depressed. She'd said, "Look at something."

I sat. Beside me, a bahia seed head angled out from its circle of grass. I picked it and studied it closely. The seed head itself was an angle, a V, two strands of tightly packed seeds tucked in at an angle. Amazing.

Across the meadow, a car door slammed, the neighbors bringing Ross back, I assumed, but when I looked up, it was Ormond.

We walked toward each other and met at the table down by the pond. We ate our lunch slowly. He spoke. I listened. I repeated what I thought he'd said. I spoke. He listened. Pat was right, we'd made progress.

Even so, it took another three weeks to decide to become a two-household family. Our close friends kidded us about how long it was taking. I didn't mind. I'd found a passage in the latest Rollo May I was reading, *Love and Will*; "It is an old and ironic habit of human beings to run faster when we have lost our way."

I took this to mean we were not, in fact, lost.

When I mentioned moving to Tallahassee, a colleague in Jerry Stern's novel workshop, Steve Watkins, told me about a house for rent in his neighborhood.

I said, "Let's go."

We jumped in his Volkswagon bus and drove out to see it, a charming three-bedroom brick house with a small screened porch surrounded by azaleas and a low picket fence. The neighborhood, Glendale, was full of graduate students, young professionals, children, live oaks, and dogwoods. I breathed the air deeply.

A few days later I took Ormond to see it. Insofar as he could like anything about the arrangement, he liked the house, the neighborhood. It felt safe; the Leon County Sheriff lived there. And Anne and Ross loved it, especially when Steve showed them a secret park with swings, seesaw, and slide tucked behind houses where no one but neighbors would know it was there.

I put my deposit and my trust once again in the hands of a realtor, my landlord, Rogers Barry, who lived across the street from the house. I didn't regret it. Even Ormond began to warm to the idea of the two-household family. "Never hold this against me in later arguments," he said one night in June, "but it might be good to have a place in Tallahassee."

On June 22 Daniel Shaughnessy of Coker, Myers & Shickel filed a Motion for Summary Judgment on behalf of the Columbia County school board. The brief outlined "the broad discretionary powers" the courts have historically granted school boards to select textbooks to be used in the curriculum, powers which even allowed boards "to make ill advised and imprudent decisions." Citing a 1980 case, *Zykan v. Warsaw Community School Corp.*, Shaughnessy pointed out that a finding of "flagrant abuse of discretion" by the school board was necessary to justify intervention by the federal courts:

> In reviewing this area of the law, it is important to note that the standards for evaluating a school board's exercise of its discretion with respect to curriculum materials is frequently treated quite differently then [sic] other forms of restriction on students' free speech.

Among the cases he cited supporting this point was *Kuhlmeier v. Hazelwood School District*, a case that would come back to haunt us. In *Kuhlmeier*—or *Hazelwood*, as some people called it—student members of a Missouri high school newspaper staff filed First Amendment action after their principal censored two pages of their publication, *Spectrum*, because the articles, in his opinion, contained potentially sensitive subjects—pregnancy and the impact of divorce on one student at school. The U.S. District Court ruled that the students' First Amendment rights had not been violated, but the Court of Appeals reversed this decision. *Hazelwood* was headed for the U.S. Supreme Court.

> For all of the reasons stated above, Defendants submit that there is no disputed issue of material fact

which would support Plaintiffs' allegations of any constitutional violation of their rights of free speech or religion and their [sic] is an utter absence of any record evidence which would indicate that level of abuse of discretion necessary to sustain their action.

In late July, as Ormond and I were moving furniture to the house in Tallahassee (the "Tallahousie," we called it), Jacobson filed our Motion for Summary Judgment. While Shaughnessey's Motion had been a brief justification for what he referred to as an "ill advised and imprudent" decision, Jacobson's was a long eloquent plea for protecting First Amendment rights in the schools:

The right to receive information and to read and learn applies of necessity with special force to the educational environment of the schools. The Supreme Court has stated expressly that the right to receive information and ideas "is 'nowhere more vital' than in our schools and universities' (*Kleindienst v. Mandel*, 1972). Still further, students must always remain free to inquire, to study and to evaluate, to gain new maturity and understanding; otherwise our civilization will stagnate and die. (*Sweezy v. New Hampshire*, 1957)."

He cited the 1982 decision in *Sheck v. Baileyville School Committee*, "Public schools are major marketplaces of ideas, and First Amendment rights must be accorded all 'persons' in the market for ideas, including secondary school students," then he continued:

The School Board seems to assert that "what the Board giveth, the Board can taketh away." But the issue is not so simplistic. These books were not the property of the board and were not given by the Board. They were purchased with public funds to be the property of the body politic, including plaintiffs. The School Board had been under no compulsion to

buy the books. But once the books became part of the
school system's collection of speech, First Amendment rights attached to them.

The rest of his brief sawed through the supports of major
school board defenses: the works "were not so pervasively
vulgar and foul as to be unfit for students old enough and/or
literate enough to understand them." The students who received "the instant materials" were high school juniors and
seniors, the latter eighteen years old which put the school board
"in the position of censoring non obscene reading material of
adults." The displeasure of students or their parents didn't
justify taking away the individual copies of all students, Jacobson
argued, quoting *Keefe v. Geanakos*, "With the greatest of respect
to such parents, their sensibilities are not the full measure of
what is proper education."

He objected to the "sweep" of the board's action:

When governmental authority is entitled to
constrict First Amendment rights, the constriction
must be the narrowest possible to accomplish the
permitted purposes. Here the School Board went the
full distance of putting the offending books under
lock and key, even though there were numerous less
severe alternatives available.

Further, he pointed out, neither work nor the humanities
course was required of students:

Overriding all else is the optionality of the
instant materials. The Humanities course was only
offered, not required. "Lysistrata" and "The Miller's
Tale" likewise were only offered, not required. No
student at Columbia High had to take Humanities,
and no student taking Humanities ever had to lay
eyes on "Lysistrata" or "The Miller's Tale" against
his or her will ... Fear by the Board that adult or
nearly adult students might choose voluntarily to
acquaint themselves with Aristophanes or Chaucer

cannot, plaintiffs fervently hope, be deemed legal grounds for suppression of a book like Volume I or of works like "Lysistrata" and "The Miller's Tale."

"More fundamentally yet," he insisted, "it is inconceivable that a school board's literary or artistic taste can be permitted total and absolute sway as to the educational materials to be permitted within the Board's jurisdiction."

Can a school board bar the Declaration of Independence or the Gettysburg Address because of the prose tastes of its members? Can a school board legally outlaw the *Scarlet Letter* because of the moral predilections of its members? ... Can a school board by operation of literary taste deny its students Sophocles as well as Aristophanes, or Shakespeare as well as Chaucer? Is there to be no First Amendment recourse against the tyranny of board taste? Can classics generally considered indispensable to education be banned because a board doesn't "like" them? To ask these questions is to answer them."

He denied that voting board members out of office was a satisfactory answer to our complaint because "book bans commonly suit the majority of the electorate." Nor did placement of one "token" copy in the school library provide "salvation" for the school board: "The availability of school-banned materials from other sources has explicitly been held insufficient justification for banning.

The forces or orthodoxy and uniformity are always at work against the impulse to individuality. History has taught us that individuality is imperiled when orthodoxy is empowered. The action of the School Board here was an imposition of orthodoxy upon the school community. The Board's action, if upheld, will have a doubly detrimental consequence of abridging the liberty of individuals and also of setting a tone of orthodoxy in the Columbia County educational system.

He cited the 1967 Supreme Court decision, *Keyishian v. Board of Regents of New York*:

> The First Amendment does not tolerate laws that cast a pall of orthodoxy over the classroom. The Nation's future depends upon leaders trained through wide exposure to a robust exchange of ideas which discovers truth "out of a multitude of tongues, [rather] than through any kind of authoritative selection."

Finally, he quoted Franklin Delano Roosevelt:

> "If the fires of freedom and civil liberties burn low in other lands, they must be made brighter in our own. If in other lands the press and books and literature of all kinds are censored, we must redouble our efforts here to keep them free. If in other lands the eternal truths of the past are threatened by intolerance, we must provide a safe place for their perpetuation."

"His words," concluded Jacobson, "remain as true today."

Nine.

On September 10, 1987, our case reached U.S. District Court. A big orange sun rose southeast of Interstate 10 as Susan and Monya and I rode to Jacksonville, Monya weaving in and out of morning rush-hour traffic in her black Lincoln Continental, a fuzzbuster prominently displayed on the dash. We wanted plenty of time to park and eat breakfast before court convened at 9:30. Our mood was optimistic: fundamentalists in Tennessee and Alabama had just been defeated in the Sixth and Eleventh Circuit U.S. Appeals Court. *Newsweek* reported that "the Fundamentalist strategy of using constitutional cases to restore religion to the school classroom looks to be in tatters." Students could now read L. Frank Baum *et al.* in Hawkins County, Tennessee, and teachers in Alabama could use the forty-four textbooks removed back in March by Judge Hand.

I brought along the article about our case from the previous day's *Lake City Reporter* and read it to Susan and Monya:

> Columbia County is not alone in attempts to censor students' freedom to learn.
> According to a report done by the People For The American Way, 153 censorship attempts in 41 out of 50 states occured during the 1986-87 school year. These incidents include charges ranging from "secular humanism" to witchcraft.

Monya laughed, "*Witchcraft?*"
"That's what it says."

"Let the woman read," Susan said.

I read on:

> We are witnessing a widening assault on the role of the schools as a place to learn a variety of ideas," said executive director for People For The American Way, Arthur J. Kropp. "Local activists supported by national censorship organizations are standing in the schoolhouse door trying to keep ideas out. These groups are pressuring teachers and librarians to eliminate materials and ideas that don't conform to their narrow views. They want schools to teach students what to think, not how to think," he said.

> A press release from the Florida Forum stated at least one third of all the textbooks used in Florida's public high schools last year were censored or "dumbed down."

> The term "dumbing down" was established by President Reagan's National Commission on Excellence in Education which reported that access to good textbooks is a significant factor in the achievement of students and limiting student access to competent texts and ideas cannot but have an injurious effect on the quality of education.

"Do tell," said Susan.

I read on and stopped. "Oh, my God."

"What?"

"It says *Goldilocks and the Three Bears* has been banned because it teaches that 'unlawful breaking and entering will go unpunished.'"

They roared. I didn't. The scene in my novel—Reverend Reymond telling Roz *The Tale of Two Bad Mice* promoted breaking and entering—was closer to fact now, not fiction.

I paid the solemn attendant at All Right Parking in downtown Jacksonville across the street from the old post office building, now the federal courthouse, a sand-colored five-story slab of a building at the corner of Pearl and Monroe. We ate breakfast at a nearby cafe and walked back to the courthouse, stopping on the steps to chat with reporters we now knew by name.

Inside the courthouse, at the end of an august hall of black and white tile and a high ornate ceiling, we passed through security clearance. Police x-rayed our purses and told us our courtroom was on the fifth floor. When the elevator stopped at the second, a winsome middle-aged man in a lightweight gray suit stepped on with us. He regarded us through silver wire-rim glasses. "You must be Mrs. Virgil, Davis, and Johnson."

It was Sam Jacobson, heretofore a voice on the phone.

Courtroom No. 2 is a large chilly room with pale gray walls and gray no-nonsense carpet. Overhead there's a white ornate ceiling decorated with eagles. Another eagle, this one brass, sits on top of a pole above a drooping American flag.

Jacobson directed us past the gallery half full of people to the front row of hard wooden benches. We sat. He unloaded two double-wide briefcases onto one of two large mahogany tables and sat in a red leather chair. At the other table, Daniel Shaughnessy stood and assembled his notes, his shoulders hunched forward, his wavy gray hair curling over his collar, his navy blue suit flecked with dandruff. Silas Pittman and board members Jack Haltiwanger and Keith "let 'em roll" Hudson sat on the bench just behind him.

I heard scratching noises behind us. A woman in a baggy beige pantsuit was sketching our picture for the news later that night. I looked away from our portrait-in-process to one on the wall—the Honorable Charles R. Scott—who looked patiently on, a little wistful, I thought, as if he wished the proceedings would start.

They finally did. The bailiff appeared in black gown and pronounced widow's peak. "Case No. 86-1030-Civ-J-14, Monya G. Virgil *et al.*, Plaintiffs vs. School Board of Columbia County, Florida, *et al.*, Defendants. All rise," he said.

As we stood, the Honorable Susan H. Black entered, a beautiful woman with long ash-blonde hair (I thought of Elizabeth Montgomery on *Bewitched*). She wished us all a good morning before she sat down.

After a brief discussion with Shaughnessy and Jacobson about the grade levels that once used the banned textbook—eleventh and twelfth, they finally agreed—she moved on to paragraph eleven of the "Stipulation as to Facts."

JUDGE BLACK: It states that the School Board voted to discontinue any future use of Volume 1 in the curriculum, and then attached is a copy of the minutes of that meeting which is Exhibit No. 7. And the minutes of the meeting on page 7 set forth the reason for the action as quote, "At the bottom the Lord's name was used in vain, and at the top of that page God's name is used in vain," and those are the reasons that the record would reflect were the reasons why, the basis of the decision. Is that agreed to?

MR. SHAUGHNESSY: Your Honor, no. If I could—

JUDGE BLACK: What is the reason?

MR. SHAUGHNESSY: Your Honor, could I have a moment to confer with my client?

JUDGE BLACK: Certainly.

After conferring with Pittman, Shaughnessy returned to the lectern and argued that the statements regarding the Lord's name referred only to Fountain.

JUDGE BLACK: No, Dr. Pittman also.

MR. SHAUGHNESSY: And then it relates the statement also of Dr. Pittman. Neither of those statements would *per se* be the reasons for action taken by the School Board.

JUDGE BLACK: What is the reason?

Shaughnessy shifted uneasily, sidestepping the issue by arguing that the reason a board member may have voted to censor the text was immaterial and irrelevant.

"Irrelevant?" I whispered to Monya and Susan.

SHAUGHNESSY: If there is some impermissible reason being assigned, there is no evidence of it in the record. Statements of Dr. Pittman during a meeting prior to a vote may reflect his own opinions or partially reflect his opinions, but they are not *per se* the action of the School Board itself."

JUDGE BLACK: So it's the defendants' position that, first of all, the reason is not material, and if it were material, the School Board had no reason?

MR. SHAUGHNESSY: Not that the School Board had no reason, but that this record reflects no explanation or reason for the School Board's action.

Jacobson responded, citing three potential grounds stated for the School Board's actions: the recommendation of its own superintendent, Dr. Pittman, that anything in which the Lord's name is used in vain is inappropriate for the classroom; the complaint upon which the School Board acted in which the complainant stated that the theme of the material was pornography and women's lib; and the complainant's belief that it was inappropriate reading for anyone, but especially mixed classes of high school students.

MR. JACOBSON: It's our position that unless and until the School Board presents some other reason for its action, that we have to assume that it decided on the basis of the complaint and the recommendation of the superintendent that it was going to do what it did. Our position is that the burden, and it's pretty clear under the law, that the burden is on the School Board to justify what it did under these circumstances.

Shaughnessy insisted that these reasons did not amount to the reasons for the acts of the board.

Black questioned whether the case, without stipulated reasons, was ripe for summary judgment. She asked Shaughnessy to suggest a means by which the record could be made complete if the reasons aren't in the record.

There was a silence.

Shaughnessy admitted to being "at a bit of a loss." He'd been operating under the assumption that the board was not required to provide reasons for its actions.

Susan and Monya and I looked at each other: the board thought they could ban books without reason?

Not amused, Judge Black recessed for fifteen minutes to give the two sides time to agree on the reasons.

Jacobson conferred with Shaughnessy then he sat beside us and whispered, "Shaughnessy wants us to agree that their reasons were that the book was not educationally appropriate because of sexual explicitness and vulgarity." We didn't agree. Neither did he. When court reconvened, he spoke first.

MR. JACOBSON: Judge, we have labored valiantly to try

to arrive at some stipulation or a stipulated statement of what we each think the Board members' reasons were. We probably agree generally, but I don't think in any reasonable period of time we'll be able to agree on mutually acceptable language. By reasonable period of time, I mean any period of time you'd be willing to wait today.

Black agreed and asked counsel to file a stipulation as to the board's reasons for banning the book. She asked Mr. Shaughnessy to begin oral argument on the motion for summary judgment, but Jacobson questioned the purpose "if the record is likely to become substantially amplified and maybe even changed by evidence."

Black agreed to set oral argument for another day but before adjourning, she addressed Shaughnessy's amazing assumption that the board did not need to justify censoring books.

JUDGE BLACK: Mr. Shaughnessy, is it your position that the School Board's discretion is absolute or is qualified?

SHAUGHNESSY: It is virtually absolute, unless and until that discretion transgresses the individual constitutional rights.

JUDGE BLACK: So if the discretion is not absolute, then why wouldn't reason be important to the resolution of this controversy?

SHAUGHNESSY: As I see the burdens going, Judge, the first very high burden is on the plaintiff to show an infringement of constitutional rights, of some individual rights, which I do not feel is shown by this record. And then, only then, will the State be permitted to come in and say, yes, perhaps we have infringed on some individual rights under the Constitution in some way, but we still should be allowed to carry forward because we have an overriding State interest. I do not see this case getting to this point.

JUDGE BLACK: Mr. Jacobson?

JACOBSON: I think it's our burden initially to show that the materials involved are First Amendment speech and that they were suppressed by these people. When we make that showing, and I think our stipulation shows that, then the burden is on them to justify the suppression.

JUDGE BLACK: Counsel need to assume in the next fifteen days, just for the sake of moving on and not having to have another delay, Mr. Shaughnessy, that either the burden has shifted or it was your burden originally.

After a few procedural questions, Jacobson reminded Judge Black that they had not done one thing they had agreed they would do—give her a copy of the book in question. Black asked the clerk to mark Volume I as a joint exhibit. Jacobson asked if she wanted Volume II.

JUDGE BLACK: Since it's here, go ahead and mark it. So Volume I will be stipulated Exhibit 1, Volume II will be Exhibit 2. Is there anything further we can do at this time?

There wasn't.

"We'll be in recess," she said.

For the next two weeks, Jacobson and Shaughnessy negotiated a list of board reasons for the removal of the humanities textbook that contained "The Miller's Tale" and *Lysistrata*:

1. The sexuality in the two selections.

2. A belief that portions of the two selections were excessively vulgar in language and subject matter, regardless of the value of the works as literary classics.

3. A belief that the subject matter of the selections was immoral, insofar as the selections involved graphic, humorous treatment of sexual intercourse and dealt with sexual intercourse out of wedlock.

4. A belief that the sexuality of the selections was violative of the socially and philosophically conservative mores, principles and values of most of the Columbia County populace.

5. A belief that the subject matter and language of the selections would be offensive to a substantial portion of the Columbia County populace.

6. A belief that the two selections were not necessary for adequate instruction in the course; nor was this particular textbook, in its entirety, necessary for instruction in the course.

7. A belief that the two selections were inappropriate to the age, maturity, and development of

the students in question.

Both Jacobson and Shaughnessy preferred this list to deposing board members. As Jacobson said to us in a letter, "They are fearful the Board members will do poorly at a deposition, and I am afraid that the members might with proper coaching be good enough to devastate us."

We were a little dismayed that he didn't attempt to include religious reasons. He agreed that these would make the case more winnable if they could be established, but he also believed that the religious element was not clear cut and could dilute our fundamental freedom of speech issue. Speech infringment, he believed, was our bedrock complaint and so he wanted the Court to answer one question: "Is school board discretion inviolable as to freedom of speech for high school students?"

Our new court date was set for December 16.

That fall we tested the two-household family. At the farm in Suwannee County, our builder, Tim Boyette, broke ground for our house. Roller skating at a friend's house in Tallahassee, Anne fell and broke four fingers. Her swollen hand looked like an inflated Rubbermaid glove. She took it well, called the cast on her hand "a good ice-breaker" at her new school, but she wasn't happy. She missed Melrose Elementary School and her father. So did Ross. He insisted he hated his primer year teacher. I bet him a quarter he'd like her by the end of the year.

I started teaching two classes in freshman composition and returned to the novel when I wasn't taking care of the kids. I felt swamped, at sea, without anchor, "without our familiar mooring places," as Rollo May said. I felt torn between an impulse to scrap the two-household idea and faith that we all would adjust if I didn't.

One day on campus Jerry Stern said, "We see less of you than we did when you lived in Lake City." He asked how I was doing. I said I felt like some kind of free-floating spore, waiting to land, put down roots. Later, I looked up the word:

> **spore**, 1. in *biology*, any of various small repro-
> ductive bodies, often consisting of a single cell ...
> they are highly resistant and are capable of giving

rise to a new adult individual, either immediately or
after an interval of dormancy. 2. any small organism
or cell that can develop into a new individual.

Well, I thought, maybe I will.

In late September Ross's teacher, Janet Braun, called. She
was concerned about Ross. His work was fine, she assured me,
but he wandered aimlessly in the classroom. "He seems lost,"
she said. I knew how he felt. We scheduled a conference.

Later that day, playing *Milles Bornes* with Ross, we talked
about how he was feeling. He said he was worried. "Daddy's
lonely without us," he said.

I asked if he was lonely without Daddy.

"Yes," he said.

"I feel that way, too." I fanned out my cards and studied
Ross from behind them. I felt guilty: I'd given him a much better
school and deprived him of time with his father, one of his finest
teachers. He was such a bright, funny kid, and now at loose
ends, thanks to me. I was, too. I loved Tallahassee, but it just
wasn't home without Ormond. I knew I'd miss him but I hadn't
realized how much I'd miss the fabric of everyday life lived
together.

Ross frowned at his cards. "Play, Mommy," he said.

I put down a go card, a green light. "You know what I'd
like?"

"What?"

"I'd like to forget the farm and Tallahassee and find a new
place where we *all* could be happy."

"Me, too," Ross said.

I played a card. "So, how could we do that? How could we
find location C?"

He looked thoughtful. "Invent it?"

At the conference at Kate Sullivan school, I asked Ms.
Braun if my volunteering would help Ross feel more at home.
She thought it might. I promised to stop at his school a few hours
each week. Ross was delighted. There I was every Thursday,
helping him and his classmates use the computer, bind books

they had written, plant beans in milk cartons.

In October we bought a piano, and Anne started lessons. Ross admitted he liked Janet Braun. They both started bringing friends home from school. While the stock market plunged on Black Monday, Anne's birthday, October 19, I made a Peter Pan costume out of green felt and took her and four friends, all in costume, to Godfather's Pizza. My teaching improved. By November, we had all turned a corner.

"Such *contentment*," I wrote in my journal.

Our life had fallen into a rhythm: on Tuesday and Thursday I taught my classes; on Monday, Wednesday, and Friday, I wrote. On Friday afternoon, I threw Anne and Ross and a pile of ungraded essays into the car and drove to the farm. On Saturday we worked on the house. On Sunday I threw Anne and Ross and a pile of half-graded essays into the car and drove back to Tallahassee. There were times I thought it was crazy, times when I quoted Thoreau in my journal, "*Simplify, simplify,*" but sometimes it felt, well, exhilarating. I felt like a pioneer of the '80s, pushing the outside of the envelope, the Chuck Yeager of fragmented living.

Court reconvened on December 16, a clear cool winter day, the kind that makes Florida famous—highs in the sixties. Susan, Monya and I met Sam Jacobson outside the courtroom. He praised our fortitude.

At two o'clock Judge Black entered and wished us a good afternoon. She acknowledged the Stipulation Concerning Board Reasons, and turned to Shaughnessy.

JUDGE BLACK: Is it still your position that the School Board has absolute discretion?

MR. SHAUGHNESSY: Let me go through that, Judge. I believe there is support for the position that the School Board has absolute discretion, when we are limiting the issue to the content of curriculum as opposed to all kinds of other issues in the cases cited such as library books, armbands as symbolic speech, that sort of thing.

JUDGE BLACK: The Pico case, the library book case, spoke of removing books after they were placed in the library. Here we have the removal of something from the curriculum after it's placed in the curriculum. And your position is that the School Board has absolute discretion to remove anything that is placed in the curriculum from the curriculum?

MR. SHAUGHNESSY: That is my position, Judge.

JUDGE BLACK: Well, wasn't this an elective course, optional reading? What's the difference between that and placing a book in the school library?

Shaughnessy acknowledged the course was elective.

JUDGE BLACK: If that's the case, did the School Board ever consider something in the area of informing the parents, as you do with movies, that some individuals in the community, their values might be offended in some parts of this course, although the course is State-approved. Was that ever considered?

MR. SHAUGHNESSY: Not considered to my knowledge, Judge.

He softened on the point of absolute discretion but still took the position that the School Board's discretion was "extremely broad" and the burden rested "upon plaintiff" to show which constitutional right was being infringed.

JUDGE BLACK: Haven't they alleged that it sharply implicates the First Amendment?

MR. SHAUGHNESSY: I think something more than that is needed in a First Amendment case. The only constitutional right that I have found identified in the cases which might even be suggested here is the right framed in the majority opinion in Pico, which is the right to receive information as opposed to the right to actually speak. While it is true under Pico that students have a right to the free flow of information and to the receipt of information, nowhere in any decision is it held that a student has the right to receipt of any information or any collection of information as a part of the curriculum which the School Board chooses. And I think that issue is pointed up in this case. The book in question has been removed from the curriculum but sits on the library shelves. It is fully available to any student who wants to read it. It is simply not available in the curriculum.

JUDGE BLACK: What governmental interest is served by placing a book in the school library that is not served by keeping it as optional reading in an elective course?

Shaughnessy, referring to the newly stipulated reasons, said the board had censored the works regardless of their literary merit because they were "somewhat vulgar, somewhat offensive, in that particular community, and as a result of that or as an additional thing they find them to be inappropriate for the age and maturity of the particular students in question."

Judge Black asked Shaughnessy to identify the particular passages that would support vulgarity or indecency.

Shaughnessy ran his hand through his hair.

MR. SHAUGHNESSY: I have a particular problem with that, Judge, in that I have neglected to bring the actual text with me.

A few people snickered.

Shaughnessy spoke *extempore* about the earthiness of "The Miller's Tale" and *Lysistrata*, then he shifted to a new set of questions: What might happen if the board lost the case? Would the Court direct the reinstatement of this book in the Humanities course? If so, for how long? Would the Court be required repeatedly to review the School Board's selection or deletion of materials in the curriculum with respect to this course or these materials and ultimately all courses and all materials? He reiterated that the Court's review is limited only to cases which show a clear implication of First Amendment rights.

Judge Black thanked him and turned to Jacobson. He carried his notes to the lectern.

JUDGE BLACK: Is it your position that the School Board's decision forecloses a particular type of thinking?

MR. JACOBSON: Thinking? It's our position that the School Board seeks to restrict and impose a certain kind of thinking on students and seeks to prohibit them from having access that might lead them to a certain type of thinking. I don't know that they can or they would purport to stop anybody from thinking, but they are certainly seeking to direct and channel the formation of people's thought processes.

JUDGE BLACK: What type of thinking?

MR. JACOBSON: I think that they're trying to affect their thinking with regard to matters of sociological philosophy, matters of personal choice, of philosophic values. Fundamentally, I think that the effort by the School Board here, whether they realized that they were doing it or not, was an effort to seek to perpetuate their own personal religiously-based philosophy as to morality, as to social values and as to matters of that sort, their own conventional orthodoxy, a kind of Protestantism and Christian ethic that they think was offended by these materials, and they wanted to stamp that out. They don't want to have that kind of material getting into the minds of the students in their high school. That's what we believe. They were upset not just by a couple of words that were used, but by the way people were expressing themselves, the things people were doing and some of the values, some of the thoughts, ideas and ways of living that they were afraid were being communicated to their students. We're not seeking to take over their curriculum structuring. They have broad curriculum, broad powers of choice with regard to curriculum and formation of curriculum and course selection and course structuring and things of that sort. But what we are saying is that they cannot exercise that discretion in the form of book banning, taking books, particularly books like these, and locking them away, prohibiting the currency of these books. School Boards may have important decisions to make of an educational sort, they're going to be made on educational bases, but when it happens that their decisions implicate constitutional values, especially preferred First Amendment type values, then they're making decisions, whether they understand or not what they're doing, they're making decisions that involve constitutional implications and its courts, its judges, who are trained and who are oriented towards issues like that and who are in a position to make the sensitive kinds of determinations, and if School Board taste, even if it's taste alone, if School Board taste contravenes First Amendment values, then the courts are brought into the picture, become implicated because it's the courts that are vested with the responsibility for making constitutional determinations.

JUDGE BLACK: Well, the defendant then brought forth in argument a parade of, I would suggest perhaps a parade of horribles, and so why don't you be specific as to the remedy and respond to his position?

MR. JACOBSON: As far as the remedy we're seeking is concerned, we ask only that you require what their own review committee made up of educational professionals wanted to do, that is put this book back in the hands of students. We're not asking that anybody be required to read it. We're just saying they need to be taken away from lock and key; that the situation of having literary material locked up by a governmental authority and not only by a governmental authority but by a School Board, then that's something that's intolerable under our Constitution. We want them to put the books back in the hands of the students and teach the course like their committee said it should be taught.

JUDGE BLACK: What if they decided that next year they didn't want to teach the course at all?

Jacobson said it was their business if they decided to cancel the class for valid educational reasons, but having seen fit to put a course in the curriculum, if they decided they didn't like these materials in the course because they express philosophic ideas they don't like, he believed they might be in trouble.

MR. JACOBSON: But I impute to the School Board good faith and I would hope if you tell them, look, you people can decide on purely educational bases devoid of ideology and things of that sort what courses you're going to teach, and if you don't want to teach this course, you don't have to, but if you drop this course because I said this book is a book that can't be banned, then you might have troubles, I think that they should heed you.

JUDGE BLACK: Well, their response is they haven't banned the book, the book is in the library.

Jacobson pointed out that it was plainly a burden on speech when materials purchased for students and placed in student hands are taken away and just one copy is placed in the library where "they have to get them on a one time basis, and they have to sign up and make their identities known, and they can only keep them for a certain period of time." This was comparable, he suggested, to the city of Jacksonville deciding the *Times Union* was tasteless and putting two or three copies in a repository in every neighborhood.

JACOBSON: I think I have the right to take the *Times Union* if I want to, and I think these students have the same right to have their own copy of these existent materials that were bought for them so they can browse through them as they wish.

JUDGE BLACK: I think that the defendants might say that you're an adult, and that these are students, and that the School Board has a right to protect the students as far as the kind of courses they should be offered. I think that would be their response.

MR. JACOBSON: Well, I don't think it would hold water. In the first place, as we've seen from the memorandum, perforce, some and probably most of these students are adults. The ones that aren't actually adults, chronologically speaking, are so close that I don't know that there is any kind of substantial difference, but even apart from all of that, students are not second class citizens who are turned over to the School Board for purposes of every kind of decision making. There are a lot of cases saying that the rights of students are particularly to be cherished, and that the First Amendment rights of students, even within that area of cherishment, are especially, we're to be especially tender of those.

JUDGE BLACK: Do you think there is any room for settlement?

MR. JACOBSON: All we want them to do is give the books back to the students. We're not saying make anybody teach these two selections or make anybody read these two selections. They can even X-rate these two selections if they want to and say, we advise you not to read them. [A few people tittered.] We won't even complain if they wanted to do that. All we're concerned about is the hard core, bedrock act of suppressing literature, and not just any literature but hallowed literature, that we say is of just manifestly First Amendment proportions.

The burden, he concluded, was now on the defendants to show some strong compelling state need to justify the suppression and to show that the suppression was the narrowest that would accomplish their purpose.

Shaughnessy rebutted by asking what ideas were being suppressed? The burden, he believed, was on plaintiff to show the suppression of ideas, either political or religious.

Black spoke for Jacobson, apologizing for using a popular term, and said the ideas suppressed were "a lifestyle different than that being promoted by the community."

Shaughnessy argued that "lifestyle" did not qualify as an idea, but was "something amorphous, something sociological. There is no idea that you can put your hand on here that is contained in Chaucer's 'The Miller's Tale' that is being suppressed. It's great literature."

Do tell, I thought to myself. I scribbled a note, a quote from Eugene Crook, a Chaucer scholar at Florida State:

> The basic moral at the end of "The Miller's Tale" is that anybody who fools around with adultery and promiscuity is going to get his ass burned in this life and the next.

I slipped it to Sam Jacobson. He read it and smiled.

Shaughnessy conceded that in the case of *Lysistrata*, one might argue that the idea of pacifism or opposition to war was being suppressed. We three nodded. "The bottom line here," he concluded, "is dictating what must be in the curriculum at the behest or upon the complaint of a parent or a small group of parents within the community."

Judge Black offered Jacobson the last word. He returned to the lectern.

MR. JACOBSON: We think that there's a wealth of idea and philosophy and value being communicated in both these works, not just with regard to a lifestyle but with regard to a philosophic stance toward war, with regard to the role of the sexes in societies or certain kinds of societies or the ways in which people who are not involved in combat are affected by war and can assert themselves with regard to war and take public positions. All of this is as far as the Aristophanes is concerned. There is just a huge communication of social value and social thought there. As far as "The Miller's Tale" is concerned, it's not just a simple earthy tale. Anybody who has read Chaucer knows that Chaucer, however primitive or earthy his language in this tale maybe have seemed compared to what we regard as more developed English, that Chaucer was a master in the formulation of stories that made points, that told things, that communicated ideas. And there's a tremendous amount communicated about love and about marriage and about sexual relationships in "The Miller's Tale." If nothing else, there's a major point communicated about sexual licentiousness in the portrayal of Absalom and what happens to him in the course of that. I should think that the School Board, in view of what is apparently their view toward sexual promiscuity, would be approving of what happened to Absalom and the point that is made by "The Miller's Tale" as to what happens to people who engage in that kind of conduct. [Scattered laughter.] We think there is just a whole broad scale expression of ideas in all of these works, and it doesn't have to be a refined, narrow kind of political idea or a specific topical kind of idea. In fact, we think that the breadth and the depth of these ideas is probably even, and I hate to quantify or make any qualitative judgments as to ideas, but we think that's more basic, more fundamental to human existence and to society than the kind of temporal ideas that Mr. Shaughnessy was talking about.

Judge Black shot Jacobson a dazzling smile and promised a decision in thirty days.

Ten.

On the fourteenth of January 1988, Black's decision due any day, I opened the *Tallahassee Democrat* and laid my head on the table.

A front page story reported the Supreme Court decision in *Hazelwood v. Kuhlmeier*, one of the cases Shaughnessy cited in his Motion for Summary Judgment. The day before—the thirteenth, as luck would have it—the Court had ruled that school authorities had not violated the Constitution when they censored the student newspaper *Spectrum*.

According to the *Supreme Court Reporter*:

> The District Court concluded that school officials may impose restraints on students' speech in activities that are "'an integral part of the school's educational function'"—including the publication of a school-sponsored newspaper by a journalism class—so long as their decision has "'a substantial and reasonable basis."' (quoting *Frasca v. Andrews*, 463 F.Supp. 1043, 1052 (EDNY 1979))... .
>
> The court held that [the principal's] action was also justified "to avoid the impression that [the school] endorses the sexual norms of the subjects" and to shield younger students from exposure to unsuitable material... . The Court of Appeals for the Eighth Circuit reversed. 795 F.2d 1368 (1986). The court held at outset that Spectrum was not only "a part of the school adopted curriculum," but also a

public forum, because the newspaper was "intended
to be and operated as a conduit for student view-
point." The court then concluded that Spectrum's
status as a public forum precluded school officials
from censoring its contents except when "'necessary
to avoid material and substantial interference with
school work or discipline ... or the rights of others.'"
(quoting *Tinker v. Des Moines Independent Community
School Dist.* (1969)).

And, as I read in the paper that morning, the Supreme Court
reversed the U.S. Court of Appeals, upholding the censorship of
"expressive speech" by school authorities. Rehnquist, Stevens,
O'Connor, Scalia, and White ruled against the students; Brennan
wrote a scalding dissent, joined by Justices Marshall and
Blackmun.

The decision cited the once fundamental principle expressed in *Tinker v. Des Moines Independent Community School
District*—"Students in public schools do not 'shed their constitutional rights to freedom of speech or expression at the schoolhouse gate'"—then severely limited it by applying the opinion
in *Bethel School District No. 403 v. Fraser* that the First Amendment rights of students in the public schools "are not automati-
cally coextensive with the rights of adults in other settings."

The Court further ruled that "[e]ducators do not offend
the First Amendment by exercising editorial control over the
style and content of student speech in school-sponsored expressive activities so long as their actions are reasonably related to
legitimate pedagogical concerns." In the Court's opinion, educators needed greater control over curriculum-related expression to achieve certain pedagogical goals "to assure that partici-
pants learn whatever lessons the activity is designed to teach,
that readers or listeners are not exposed to material that may be
inappropriate for their level of maturity." The students in
Hazelwood were as young as fourteen, although the Court felt
obliged to consider the ages of "younger brothers and sisters"
who might pick up the student newspaper at home.

I slapped my forehead. Now here was a brave new standard for deciding what high school students could read—

siblings and serendipity. It was dumbing down at its worst, *carte blanche* for the censors.

Brennan, too, was dismayed, his dissent sharply worded:

> The case before us aptly illustrates how readily school officials (and courts) can camouflage viewpoint discrimination as the "mere" protection of students from sensitive topics. It is much more likely that the objectionable article was objectionable because of the viewpoint it expressed: It might have been read (as the majority apparently does) to advocate "irresponsible sex."

I was impressed by Brennan's insight—he might have been quoting Fritz Fountain—but discouraged that the rest of the Court was not as insightful.

I had departed District Court in December optimistic about Judge Black reinstating the humanities textbook. Now that didn't seem possible.

Susan and Monya disagreed. There was too great a difference between the ages of the students involved, they believed, and between student "expressive activities" and what Jacobson had called "hallowed" classics.

Sixteen days later, as I finished the penultimate chapter of the first draft of my novel, Monya called from Lake City and said in a whisper, "We lost." According to a mole in her office, Judge Black had been writing a decision in our favor, but after *Hazelwood v. Kuhlmeier* she reversed herself and ruled for the school board:

> In light of the recent decision of the United States Supreme Court in *Hazelwood School District v. Kuhlmeier*, 56 U.S.L.W. 4079 (U.S. January 13, 1988), this Court need not decide whether the plurality decision in *Pico* may logically be extended to optional curriculum materials. *Kuhlmeier* resolves any doubts as to the appropriate standard to be applied whenever a curriculum decision is subject to First Amendment review.

Precedents like *Tinker* and *Pico* ("school officials may not remove books for the *purpose* of restricting access to the political
ideas and social perspectives discussed in them, when that action
is motivated simply by the officials' disapproval of the ideas
involved") were swept aside by the sixteen day-old decision:

> The Court agrees with the plaintiffs that the
> School Board's decision reflects its own restrictive
> views of the appropriate values to which Columbia
> High School students should be exposed. The Court
> finds, however, that such content-based decision-
> making regarding curriculum is permissible under
> the standards set forth in *Kuhlmeier*. The Court in
> *Kuhlmeier* held that educators may limit both the
> 'style and content' of curricular materials if their
> action is reasonably related to legitimate pedagogi-
> cal concerns.

Black further held that denying students access to "potentially
sensitive topics" such as sexuality was a legitimate pedagogical
end and "the uncontroverted justification for the School Board's
decision in the present case," concluding that "this Court need
only consider whether the decision of the School Board was
reasonably related to this goal":

> The Court faces a number of difficulties in
> making this determination. First, the Court finds it
> difficult to apprehend the harm which could con-
> ceivably be caused to a group of eleventh- and
> twelfth- grade students by exposure to Aristophanes
> and Chaucer. Indeed, authorities on Western litera-
> ture are virtually unanimous in their high praise for
> the works of these authors.
>
> Second, the Court has a more general concern
> regarding the breadth of measures that may be taken
> to protect the students from materials containing
> sexuality or vulgarity. The plaintiffs argue in this
> case that the School Board's decision to remove
> Volume I in its entirety, rather than to take the less

drastic measure of warning students of the potentially sensitive nature of two particular works, violates the established first amendment principle that restrictions on speech must be "narrowly tailored" to achieve the government's legitimate interests. Under the standard set forth in *Kuhlmeier*, however, a School Board's decision to remove curricular materials will be upheld if it is reasonable, even where that decision is not the least restrictive of student speech. Thus, under *Kuhlmeier*, this Court assumes the limited role of determining whether sexuality or vulgarity are at all present in the removed materials, and if so, determining whether the measure taken to remove the sexuality and vulgarity was at all reasonable.

Black found both elements "unquestionably present" in the contested material. She concluded:

Although the Court wishes that the Board had imposed its standards in a manner less restrictive of speech, the Court recognizes that the Board retains broad discretion under our constitutional system in dealing with such potentially sensitive topics. As stated by the Supreme Court in *Hazelwood School District v. Kuhlmeier*, "the education of the Nation's youth is primarily the responsibility of parents, teachers, and state and local school officials, and not of federal judges." The Court will therefore grant the defendants' Motion for Summary Judgment.

It occurred to me in a slow-burn gag kind of way that we'd been the victims of board arrogance: if Pittman *et al.* had not been so cocky back in September, so convinced that they didn't need reasons for banning the textbook, we would not have delayed for three months and Black would have ruled in our favor.

Jacobson wasn't upset. He was confident that the 11th Circuit Court of Appeals would rule that *Hazelwood* had been misapplied. "This isn't over," he said. "The fat lady hasn't sung yet."

He filed a Notice of Appeal on February 19. Three days later the Supreme Court refused to hear the Tennessee case, letting stand the decision by the U.S. Court of Appeals that put *The Wizard of Oz* and other books back in the schools.

Encouraged as I was by this news, Blacks' decision still darkened my mood:

> The past few days: foul. Almost thirty-seven (almost forty, I keep thinking), teaching grade-happy freshman one of whom pointed out that I had split an infinitive while I spoke to the class. I do not want to do this. I cannot even summon the "this is a character-building experience" attitude I had last semester. I am poor. Anne needs new clothes; it took the two of us almost half an hour to put together a decent outfit—jeans, a good shirt, my old navy turtleneck. She left looking wonderful; I felt close to tears. I am bogged down at the end of the two-year-long-now first draft of the novel. The teaching, two households, home-building, single-parenting are encroaching on the writing I want to do. Avalanche imagery applies. I am deeply uncertain about living in Suwannee County but I am ready to simplify my life to the point of boredom.

In late February I flew to Tucson for a production of my play *Aspirations* and returned to find my phone disconnected. My check apparently had been delayed due to Presidents' Day. I did not have the money to pay the reconnect fee, but I was spared the expense by the kindness of strangers—the woman at the phone company said I was an excellent customer and reinstated my service.

The bright spot in the spring was our new house. After seven months' meticulous work, it was almost complete; Ormond would move there from Mildew Haven in a couple of weeks. I walked through on the morning of March 9 and admired the high ceilings, tie-beams, skylights, the porches, the yellow pine woodwork and floors. I told Ormond it was everything I thought art should be—full of light and beautifully crafted.

He said, "Come live here with me."
I said, "I don't know."

The next morning, March 10, was a work of art, too, though it didn't start out that way. I woke up oppressed by the choice I had to make before the school year was over—continue the two-household family or move to Suwannee County.

"Death or chi-chi," I wrote in my journal.

I felt oppressed by all I had to accomplish that day: wake, feed and clothe the kids and put them on the bus, pick up tiles for the bathrooms at the new house, prepare and teach my two classes, make an appointment with Jerry Stern to discuss the last chapter of the first draft of my novel, pick up the kids at after-school care, prepare the speech about our censorship case (now called *Virgil et al.*) and give it that night to the Tallahassee chapter of the A.C.L.U.

I knew I had to get up and get moving so I lay there in bed and listened to NPR recite the election results from Super Tuesday. Pat Robertson had been soundly defeated—another flop for the Fundamentalist Follies. This inspired me to get out of bed and make coffee.

I woke Anne and Ross, took a shower, and made us all breakfast. We dressed and walked to the bus, then I drove down to campus where I worked on my classes and saw Jerry Stern. He liked the last chapter but he thought it needed some work. We made an appointment for nine the next morning.

I walked into class that afternoon, both guns blazing. I had never been so prepared. "This is hard!" my students exclaimed. "We have to think!" I realized I was having a wonderful time.

So were the kids. When I picked them up at after-school care, Anne told me she'd won at checkers; Ross had triumphed at kickball. We piled in the car and hurtled up and down Sixth Street past the azaleas and houses of Lafayette Park to our house on Laurel.

I changed mental cassettes, as I'd come to call it, though on days like this it felt more like hitting scan on the car radio— mother turns teacher turns mother turns public speaker. I fed the kids and worked on my speech. We ate dinner. The baby-sitter came and I went.

My speech went surprisingly well. Afterward, two lawyers presented me with a copy of their forthcoming article, "Tinkering With *Tinker*: Academic Freedom in the Public Schools After *Hazelwood School District v. Kuhlmeier*." The chair of the statewide A.C.L.U. invited me to speak at their annual meeting in Tampa the following fall.

I drove home delighted that I had salvaged the day. Maturity is its own reward, I decided. Anne and Ross were still awake so I told them how well it had gone, then I tucked them in bed and kissed them goodnight. I was too wired to sleep. I turned on the basketball game, Indiana's arch rival Purdue vs. Ohio State. I called Ormond so he could watch, too.

While Ohio State whipped Purdue, I read "Tinkering With *Tinker*." Like Jacobson, the authors argued that *Virgil* was not best decided by applying *Hazelwood*. I went to bed hoping the U.S. Court of Appeals would agree.

The next morning I was in a wonderful mood. When Anne and Ross left for school, I hopped in the car to head down to campus. My landlord was sweeping leaves off his sidewalk, so I stopped and rolled down the window. He asked if I'd decided to stay or go back to the country. I told him I hadn't made up my mind. "Be careful," he said, "There are mean people there."

I laughed. "You said a mouthful there, fella."

He said he had something for me, a pot of flowers—Red Flame—to hang on my porch. I thanked him and drove on to campus.

Jerry Stern and I met in his office and went line by line through my last chapter. He thought the "ravening mob" that burned Roz's house to the ground was a little far-fetched. I chuckled, agreeing, and made a note to cut the house-burning scene.

After our meeting, I drove to the mall to buy Tylenol. I had no idea how badly I'd need it.

When I got home, the light was blinking on my answering machine. I flipped it on and heard Ormond's voice.

"Claudia, our house burned down. Call me."

Eleven.

If I said this hit like a sledge in the gut, I would not be overstating the case, but I knew it had hit Ormond harder.

Yes, we'd worked together finding the land, an architect, a builder, and financing construction; we'd worked on the house every weekend, and though there were times I felt real elation—singing show tunes together while we stained the trim boards—I knew it was his house, not ours.

For seven months he had driven to the site twice a day—at lunch and again after work—to check on details, the slow progress. He had made all the on-site decisions, discovered the screw-ups, dogged the crew until it was right. He had planned to move into the house in two weeks.

The red light blinked dumbly at me. I thought, they should code these things for good and bad news. I thought, this isn't true. I thought, it could have been arson, the fundamentalist backlash he feared from the start? *They'll be burning crosses on our front yard.*

I called Ormond at work. When he answered the phone I started to cry. All I could say was, "This can't be happening." He said calmly, "It already has."

What happened was this:

Some time after seven, while the children and I were eating our breakfast in Tallahassee, Ed Bailey, a neighbor in Suwannee County, drove to work past our land and saw a thin column of smoke rising from the southwest corner of our new house. The morning was cold, a stiff northeasterly wind, so he figured it was one of the workers building a fire to keep his hands warm. Later, when he heard that our house had burned down, it hit him that our gate had been locked.

Sometime around eight, while I was walking the kids to the bus, the foreman Ronnie drove out to the site. A half-mile away he saw the fire and thought, *it could be their house*. He roared up the road, saw the locked gate, saw the fire curling up through the roof, spun his truck around in the sand and drove to the first house on the road, Alma Bailey's, where he screeched to a stop, jumped out of the pickup, tripped, and fell into the bushes.

Inside the house, Alma Bailey was watching. She didn't know the man in her bushes. She figured he was drunk or crazy or both. When he stumbled onto her porch and started knocking, she didn't open the door. Ronnie ran back to his truck and drove to the preacher's house out on the hard-top. His hand was shaking so hard the preacher had to dial the fire department.

Sometime around nine, as Jerry Stern said the house-burning scene in my novel was a little far-fetched, Christine Bailey, Ed's wife, called Ron Ceryak at the Water Management District and asked how she could get hold of Ormond. Ron called Ormond at work and told him what Christine had said: there was a fire out at our place.

By the time Ormond got there the flames were eighty feet high, a bonfire of cypress and pine. He stood by the shed and watched it burn down. The master carpenter, David Stevens, a big burly man, sat with his shaggy head in his hands and cried like a baby. Tim Boyette threw up. Ormond went into a mild state of shock.

On the phone, I mistook this for calm. Standing there in my small house in Tallahassee, I asked what we were going to do. Ormond said he thought he'd go on to his professional meeting down in Orlando.

I said, "You *can't*."

He said, "What's the point of sticking around? We'll just be unhappy together."

So deep in shock I couldn't see his, I called my friend Jan in Lake City. I told her what happened. I told her Ormond was planning to go to Orlando. "If he goes to that meeting," I said, "I'll file for divorce."

Jan, who recognized shock—his and mine—where I couldn't, said with genuine calm, "You can't expect him to do what you haven't asked him to do. You're assuming he knows what you need."

I called him back but I didn't have to tell him he had to stay home, wherever that was. While Jan had been counseling me, his staff had gathered around and comforted him. They urged him not to go to his meeting. They gently suggested that he was in shock. They told him he and I needed each other.

He told me he was leaving for Tallahassee.

Friends and neighbors brought food, the Southern sympathy card. We were grateful. Some stayed to talk. We talked about arson, Abernathy, the censorship case. No, someone said, construction fires were common. Ormond said our crew had been careless, smoking cigarettes while they sawed wood on the porch in ankle-deep sawdust.

In the late afternoon, when friends and neighbors were gone and Anne and Ross went out to play—glancing back at the house; they were worried about us—we talked about how hard it had been to hold up our end of polite conversation. We were lost in the loss, thinking about the house burning down, then we'd realize someone was talking to us and we'd tune back in only to drift off again. I thought of what Jan had told me when her father died: her life went on automatic pilot. She went through the motions but was not really there.

By early evening, our emotional immune system began to kick in. We began to consider the small consolations: it was only a structure. Our stuff wasn't in it. No one had died. And we had an opportunity to do it again. Build it better. Fix those mistakes we'd discovered too late. Build bigger porches. Ormond called the burned house "a first draft."

We ate dinner and drove across town to Anne's gifted arts and crafts fair, a pavilion of student exhibits. We both stopped and stared at a group of small model houses that lit up inside.

Driving home, I stopped at Jax Liquor to buy a bottle of scotch. "In case we need it," I said. Inside, I picked up a bottle of scotch and carried it to the cash register. I told the clerk our house had burned down.

"Oh, I've been there," she nodded. "Barely got out with the shirts on our backs."

I asked if she thought we'd bought enough liquor.

She eyeballed the 1.75 liter bottle. "Not hardly," she said.

The next morning, Saturday, we drove back to the farm.

I was enraged, denial yielding to anger. We'd lost our house because of arson or carelessness, a mean redneck or a dumb one, I snarled. I was scared. I didn't know what I would see or how I would feel when I saw it.

Ormond drove. When he turned in the drive, I dug my fingers into my palm. He drove past the pines we had planted, and then, there it wasn't: no house at all, just a big bed of ashes and a charred bathtub pointing north by northwest.

Tim Boyette arrived. He told us the house had burned on his birthday, the "second candle" he got for the day. We set up three lawn chairs and watched men from M.A.S.A.—fire-and-arson experts from Tampa—walk through the ashes. They hunkered down, held up wires and other bits of debris, dusted off ashes with whisk brooms. Smoke rose from the soles of their black rubber boots. Now and then, their boots sizzled.

I told Howard Wright, Live Oak's fire marshall, about the censorship case, how I'd made people angry ("Delta is ready"), but the crew found no sign of arson, no fuses, no petroleum products. The cause of the fire, they finally decided, was a faulty extension cord in what would have been Anne's new bedroom, the northeast side of the house, though Ed Bailey swore the thin column of smoke he had seen Friday morning was rising from the opposite corner.

Tim assured us if it was arson, someone would eventually talk. He asked if we planned to rebuild.

We didn't know.

Mother Nature, that great seductress, did all she could to persuade us to build the house over again. The dogwoods were blooming, the sky was a deep cloudless blue, and while we sat overlooking the ashes, three white-tailed deer bounded by.

We spent that night and Sunday in Tallahassee. I woke up angry again, this time overwhelmed by the feeling that the farm had been nothing but trouble and loss—road, pond, and house. Ormond and I sat long-faced most of the morning as he had feared we would do.

Absorbing our tension, Ross moaned, "I don't *feel* good." Ormond slapped his knees and said he had to get back to Lake City. I panicked. I couldn't get through the day without him, with the children. I suggested taking the kids to the Junior Museum. Ormond said no, he had too much to do—feed the dog, water the pecan trees at the farm—so I resorted to guilt: Anne and Ross and I stayed late at the farm every Sunday. Ormond agreed to stay longer. I packed a picnic. And Mother Nature did it again—dogwoods and easter-green grass and a glorious day—cool and clear, in the sixties.

At the museum, the otters put on a show. They had us in stitches with their goofball routine, sliding in and out of their pool. They raced up to the fence and stood on hind legs and nodded their heads, their curtain call. Ross said what I was feeling, what he thought they were saying: "Thank you, thank you, thank you," he said.

The four of us wandered along the sand paths. We saw bobcats, red and gray foxes, more deer, bears, Florida panthers, alligators and turtles. For the first time in months I felt deeply content. I'd brought the children here numerous times but it never felt right. I told Ormond I thought we should rebuild the house.

"No," he said, "I don't have the strength."

I said, "Let's build it together."

That night I wrote in my journal:

> Sunday evening. Calm has settled in with the decision to rebuild the house. I talked to Rogers' wife, Ambers, who brought us more food. She said how good it was for the children to see that horrible things could happen to people and they went on. I thanked her for that.
>
> Tonight, O. has gone back. I caught myself singing while I made taco salad for Anne and beanie weenie for Ross, our standard short-order kitchen. I stopped and said to the kids: We're like the Who's

down in Whoville—what we had has been taken away, but we're singing.

Small blessings: The next week was spring break, so we were able to spend it together.

Ormond had out-patient surgery on his left hand to remove a splinter that had lodged under his knuckle when he sanded some trim boards before the house burned. He came back from the surgeon and unwrapped a small piece of gauze. Inside was the splinter, a half-inch of wood. He planned to save it, the only piece of the house that hadn't been destroyed by the fire. We joked about making a small reliquary: the splinter, a charred piece of cypress, a chip of tile from the bathroom, melted glass from the windows.

We began what would be a three-month ordeal of computing the quantifiable part of the loss—filing claims and rebidding the house (cypress had gone up in price; so had copper wire) with our builder and banker and insurance agent, sorting out who owed what to whom. Not one of them had been through this before.

On March 15 I wrote in my journal:

> What I know about loss is it's sudden and irreversible. It doesn't render us powerless but it throws our powerlessness in our faces. This triggers shock, disbelief, rage. Today I woke up with a sense of the monumental task, the hassle, we're faced with. I must acknowledge I won't write for a while.
>
> Loss incurs other losses. I feel addled. I lost my down vest yesterday, had to think hard where I'd left it, and I found it again, but it's real, the loss of concentration. Loss tells us it's a dangerous world and with this loss of focus, it is. Jerry says Roz needs more internal screaming. Now I know why, how it feels: pressure in the neck, behind the ears, a stabbing headache in the upper right side of my head, unabated by aspirin. Yet, at the center, in the heart and the stomach, there's a hollowed out feeling, an awareness of our vulnerability, the unbearable light-

ness of being: a cavity.

March 16 was my birthday. My father and mother and sister called, but I didn't feel happy, in fact, I couldn't stop crying. "I'm a wreck," I told my sister. "I'm having the break-down I should have had five days ago."

She said, "You couldn't have afforded it then."

The next day the Richards and Kings drove up to the farm to see what was left of the house. They were shattered, too, by the fire. We walked around the rectangle of ashes.

"Look," Sharon said, pointing. Green shoots were push-ing up through the ashes.

Ten days later, on March 27, Ormond and I celebrated our twelfth anniversary. We felt like survivors. We spent the day looking for a larger rental house where we could all live to-gether when the school year was over. We found one, a sprawl-ing ranchburger right down the road from Susan Davis. We moved Ormond in.

I was irrationally fond of this big tacky house. It was like a country-western song—short on taste, long on heart—the house where we finally got back together. The floor plan re-minded me of my life in Lake City—long and strung out. The bedrooms were flung so far from the kitchen we joked about renting a golf cart. The den had dark paneled walls and Styrofoam beams and bordello-red carpet—the Pizza Hut room, Ormond called it. It made Anne think of *Clue*, the room where Mrs. Peacock did it with the revolver.

There was a pool in the back yard under the pines but it was full of slimy green water. The realtor promised to hire a pool service to clean it. Sure enough, a pool-service truck appeared in our driveway, and, as small towns would have it, the man who slid out of the seat was Dickie Chappell, the chair of the school board that banned the humanities textbook.

In April, Sam Jacobson filed our appeal:

The determination by the District Court here that this case is controlled by *Hazelwood School Dis-*

trict v. Kuhlmeier was incorrect. The District court seriously misinterpreted and overapplied *Hazelwood*. *Hazelwood* dealt with a greatly different set of considerations. There the Supreme Court held merely that a school board was not required to publish objectionable student writings in a school newspaper. The Supreme Court gave no indication whatever in *Hazelwood* that it intended to give school boards the right to ban esteemed works by acclaimed adult authors. *Hazelwood* does not advert to book banning issues. The District Court's reading of *Hazelwood* would deprive the courts of virtually any review of school board book bans and would altogether countermand *Pico*. The Supreme Court would not have taken so huge a step without express articulation of its intent to do so.

He reframed our argument, reminding the U.S. Court of Appeals that the "Board's action, if upheld, will have the consequence not only of abridging the liberty of individuals and setting a tone of orthodoxy in Columbia County, but also of opening the way to similar erosions in all school districts which look to the federal courts for First Amendment protection."

In early May, while I was writing the second draft of the novel, Susan Davis called with what she described as "a shit-eating grin" on her face. Eighteen organizations had filed briefs of *Amici Curiae* on our behalf with the Eleventh Circuit Court of Appeals. These included, ironically, the American Association of University Women and the American Association of University Professors, although the Lake City chapter of A.A.U.W. and Lake City Community College had never expressed their support.

The argument of the *Amici Curiae* centered on the board's suppression of ideas:

The Supreme Court has repeatedly required school boards to manage school affairs and inculcate values in a manner that is "consistent with fundamental constitutional safeguards" *Tinker v. Des Moines Indep.*

Community School Dist., 393 U.S. 503, 507 (1969).
Central among those safeguards is the rule that the
First Amendment "does not permit the official suppression of *ideas*." *Pico*, 457 U.S. at 871 (plurality
opinion) (emphasis in original).

Hazelwood had affirmed only the authority of school officials to prescribe "'the boundaries of socially appropriate behavior' by students in official school settings," and provided
"little if any guidance for assessing the propriety of a school
board's decision to remove a textbook from the curriculum ... It
did not and could not, in light of its facts, signal an overruling
of the First Amendment prohibition on the censorship of ideas."

"A stone has been lifted off of my back," Susan said. "Now
I know I'm not crazy."

Most important, most satisfying, was the Florida Department of Education's decision to file in our favor. Education
Commissioner Betty Castor sided with us because our case
involved a state-approved textbook. She believed that Black
had been "overbroad" in the authority she granted to the school
board. She was also concerned about Florida's growing reputa-
tion as a censorious state:

> Book banning flies in the face of what we are trying
> to do to give the best possible curriculum. Our
> process for approving books is comprehensive. If we
> have a fault, it's that I don't think we have been
> aggressive enough in requiring higher standards.

It was the first time in recent history that the state of Florida had
opposed a local school board in a lawsuit over textbook selection.

Stung by Castor's remarks, Silas Pittman replied, "If the
school board doesn't have the right to determine the use of any
textbook—state-adopted or not—there is something wrong in
this country."

But callers responding to the latest question in the "Columbia Consensus" did not agree:

Should the state Department of Education join in the lawsuit

against the county School Board concerning textbooks local
officials have decided against using?
YES 56% NO 44%
(18 responses)

> Yes, I'm appalled that the School Board would de-
> cide under the pressure of such a few as opposed to
> so many. Yes, the DOE should join in the lawsuit,
> because once again a Columbia County Board of
> elected officials has shown what enormous ignora-
> muses they can be. This election ought to be fun. I
> hope anybody on the School Board and the County
> Commission is running in my district, because they
> are gone, gone, gone. Yes, absolutely, in banning
> such fine classical literature from Columbia County
> classrooms, the School Board looked like a group of
> illiterate idiots. Yes, it's one of the safest ways of
> fighting some of the bigotry that we have to put up
> with. Absolutely, it's time the School Board under-
> stands that people with more education and wider
> jurisdiction agree with the solid citizens that are op-
> posed to censorship in our town. Yes, of course they
> should. Everyone should be concerned with censor-
> ship, particularly of the classics. Yes, if the Depart-
> ment of Education can help us, great, we need it ....

Although fewer callers had responded, the numbers, for the
first time, were in our favor.

But there were plenty of people who were angry at us for
protesting the ban. After numerous interviews, a reporter for
the *Orlando Sentinel* concluded:

> Friction between outsiders and locals runs deep.
> Many in Lake City grumble that the ruckus would
> have died if not for persistent meddling by people
> who do not have local roots. The mothers who sued
> have lived in Columbia County less than eight years.

Anonymous phone calls started again, ranging from silence to anger. "I saw your name in the paper," one man snarled, then slammed down the phone. Others told us to keep that "perversion" out of the classroom.

Meanwhile, the Florida legislature was contributing to the state's censorious status, approving a ban on obscene bumper stickers. The "bad bumper sticker" bill, offered by Rep. Tom Banjanin, R-Pensacola, was designed to protect children from obscenity, including references in words or pictures, to sex, bestiality, excretion, deviant sexual behavior, rape or simulated sexual acts.

"What effect does that have on the psychic development of a child?" Banjanin asked his fellow lawmakers.

The next time we went to the pediatrician, his wife said the bumper sticker ban had enraged her. "What's obscene? I think it's obscene when people put their religious beliefs on the bumper!" She showed me a copy of the telegram she'd sent to the state legislature and her new membership card in the A.C.L.U.

In June, shortly after Shaughnessy filed the Appelees' Answer Brief, just before we broke ground again at the farm, Tim Boyette asked if we wanted him to bury the ashes or haul them away. We said, "Haul them away." It seemed important to have a clean start. It seemed important to avoid remarks we had made while we built the first house: "If we could do this over again ... " It seemed important to excise certain words from our vocabulary: *Burned out. Room to burn. That burned me up.* This house, we agreed, would never have a housewarming.

In late June, the phlox and black-eyed Susans in bloom, Tim prepared the new site. Ormond and I drove up to the farm to see how it looked. There it was, the second draft of our house, outlined with stakes and string. To the west, the meadow needed mowing. To the east, the blackberries needed picking. Ormond and I flipped for the tractor (we both love to drive it); he won the toss. He mowed the meadow while the children and I picked blackberries. Later, my bucket half full, I looked across the new house site and caught Ormond's eye as he rumbled past on the tractor. He lifted his straw hat, I lifted mine, and we telegraphed to each other: this house is ours.

Twelve.

The U.S. Court of Appeals, Eleventh Circuit, based in Atlanta, agreed to travel to Jacksonville to hear our case on September 15.

"The Appeal mobile," Ormond called it.

Until it arrived, we swam in the pool Dickie Chappell had cleaned and worked on the second draft of the house. Tim fired the foreman and most of the crew and put the master carpenter David Stevens in charge. David worked quietly, steadily, with one assistant named Jimbo. Tim assured us we could move in by Thanksgiving. We took this to mean, with luck, maybe Christmas. The summer passed uneventfully until August 2, a sweltering afternoon, when Jim Virgil went jogging around the cow pasture in back of his house and collapsed from a stroke. When he didn't return at the usual time, Monya stepped outside to see what had happened. Jim staggered into the garage, his legs torn and bleeding from a barbed-wire fence he'd crossed in a frantic attempt to get home.

The president of Idaho Timber flew in from Boise to guide production at the Lake City plant during Jim's hospitalization which lasted, remarkably, only two weeks. Susan and I sat with Monya, who told us the stroke had been mild; most of the damage had been to his speech.

"Par for the course in Lake City," I said.

A week after Jim returned home, when he was working hard to rebuild his speech but he was still coming up with the wrong noun at times, the president summoned him into the office at Idaho Timber and said he was fired. "A change in management" was the euphemism of choice. Jim looked at him and got the noun right. "You *bastard*," he said; nevertheless, he was out of a job.

So, in early September, was Silas Pittman. Voters were furious about a nineteen percent raise the board had awarded him shortly after the book ban. Others were angry, I would like to believe, about his pig-headed stand in the censorship fight. He was soundly defeated by a high school math teacher, Michael Flannigan, who would run against the Republican candidate, Dianne Lane, in November.

A lame duck, Pittman appeared in court on September 15. Monya and Susan and I traveled again to the Federal Building in Jacksonville and joined Sam Jacobson in the Court of Appeals Courtroom, a long narrow room overlooking All Right Parking. Three black-robed judges were listening to a reckless driving case about a runaway pickup truck, a Dixified version of Mr. Toad's ride. The judges—male, gray, in their fifties—sat behind nameplates: Tuttle, Tjoflet, and Anderson.

When the first case ended, the judges recessed. When they returned, Judge Elbert Tuttle, who had a long history of sensitivity to the First Amendment, was not among them. He had been replaced by an Alabaman, Judge Cox, who, Jacobson explained, was more of a technician, a man predisposed to side with the establishment. And Tjoflet, he whispered, was an unabashed authoritarian who disapproved of *any* nonconformist activity.

"Like three women standing up to a school board?"

Sam nodded.

"So," I asked, "is that it?"

"Well," he said, "it's a blow."

Our time in appeals court was blessedly brief. The acoustics were awful. Several times the judges cupped a hand to their ear and snapped at soft-spoken Sam, "Speak up, I can't hear you!"

One exchange rekindled my optimism: shortly before court adjourned Judge Anderson questioned Shaughnessy about the legitimacy of removing the two classics from the curriculum because they included references to sexuality.

JUDGE ANDERSON: Doesn't your argument mean that

boards might ban any work that referred to sexuality, say, *Romeo and Juliet*?

Shaughnessy admitted it might.

JUDGE ANDERSON: Isn't sexuality, being part of life, going to be part of most great literature?

Shaughnessy admitted it was.

Anderson's implication was clear: when books are banned on sexual grounds, all great literature is endangered. When books are censored on sexual grounds, any author could get screwed, but then, judging from the look on Sam's face, so were we.

In October, I told the story of *Virgil et al.* to the statewide meeting of the A.C.L.U. When I finished, people rose quickly to leave. Oh, great, I've bored them, I thought—then I realized it was a standing ovation.

For the rest of the fall, the second draft of the house and my novel took shape. Jim Virgil found a job in Couer d'Alene, Idaho, where he and Monya moved in early December. Before they left, Monya—ace of copier—gave me a large three-ring notebook with every piece of *Virgil's* documentation in chronological order and our First Commandment inscribed on the front: THOU SHALT NOT CENSOR.

Ormond and I spent the cool clear days of December staining cypress boards for our new house's siding. Our carpenter, David Stevens, and his assistant, Jimbo, hung the drywall and trimmed the windows and doors in pale yellow pine. Crews came and went, installing carpets and cabinets, the tension mounting as we approached the point in the construction when the first house had burned. Ormond camped out at the farm for a couple of nights to make sure it didn't happen again.

A few days before Christmas, the day before the final inspection, David called me out on the porch. The covers for the mounts for our fans didn't fit: our ceilings were angled; these were for flat. I asked him to jury-rig something so we could move in before Christmas. He dug in the heels of his boots. "I don't give a damn about no inspection, I want it done *right*."

I couldn't help smiling. When the first draft of the house was under construction, Ormond had dogged the foreman and crew about keeping the quality high; now, with David in charge, he was snapping at us.

I deferred to his fine sense of craft; he solved the problem with wedges of wood, and the house passed inspection. We moved in on Christmas Eve eve.

January 6, 1989:

The hooded mergansers have come to the pond, migrating north to Nova Scotia. They are small ducks with yellow eyes and straight thin pointed bills. The female is brown, nondescript, but the male has a dramatic crest on its head, a white triangle bordered by black. Their hoarse grunts and chatter are winter's answer to summer's booming chorus of frogs.

I have discovered a new capacity for joy— watching things grow—kids, trees—I'll plant longleaf pines here tomorrow. I want a raised-bed kitchen garden, strawberries, an asparagus patch.

The view from my desk here in the loft is as lovely as I expected—a sweep left to right across the three windows from our hill har har de har to the pecans Ormond planted, our shed, and the pinetrees we planted. Lo, beyond our young pines I see Ed Bailey's pasture, his cattle lowing.

News: Bobby Abernathy has moved to Atlanta. This could mean several things but probably doesn't. It means we are more tenacious than he is.

Polishing chapter 14 of the second draft of the novel. Should finish it soon.

The "Go Bulldogs" sprayed on car windows in Live Oak beginning to fade, their second state championship now a thing of the past. An Episcopalian minister in Tallahassee told friends in church, "I wish they cared as much about God in Live Oak as they do about football."

I have never loved a home quite so much— even the cabin in Indiana. It was wonderful, our first home, but we knew we'd be leaving. My feeling today: I'll never leave. I'm in my loft writing this, "The Messiah" is playing on NPR, and a turkey buzzard flies finger-feathered out over the pines.

On January 11, I added this note:

Ormond sitting in the platform rocker this morning, gazing east toward the mist on the pines. "Don't disturb me," he said, "I'm in heaven."

Two days later, paradise was temporarily lost. It was Friday the thirteenth, a year after the Supreme Court ruled in *Hazelwood v. Kuhlmeier*. I opened the Tallahassee *Democrat* and saw the headline: COURT SAYS BOARD MAY BAN BOOK:

A federal appeals court Thursday upheld the right of the Columbia County school board to discontinue the use of a textbook because of concerns about its sexual content, but seriously questioned the wisdom of the board's action.

A ruling in U.S. District Court, affirmed by the 11th Circuit, found that the decision was constitutional, given the sexuality in the two selections and the excessively vulgar language and subject matter. The board's decision, the lower court found, was within the bounds of legitimate pedagogical concerns.

Though affirming the constitutional legality of the board's decision, the court said it did not endorse the move.

Beyond frustration, I called Sam Jacobson and raved about a court allowing the banning of a textbook—thrice approved by state educators—by school board members whose expertise ranged from selling softballs to super-chlorinating a pool. The majority had probably not even *read* it.

Sam listened patiently, then pointed out that pedagogy can also include the inculcation of moral and community values.

"That's indoctrination," I said.

"Yes, which is why we are fighting it." He had every

intention of asking the Supreme Court for a writ of *certiorari*. "But don't expect this Supreme Court to help you," he added, "and if you voted for Nixon or Reagan, you have no room to complain." "I didn't," I snapped. "That's Susan and Monya."

He said he'd send the decision as soon as he got a copy.

That night I drove to the Richards' house down by Ichetucknee Springs and played cards with Sharon and Jan. Sharon said she was sorry we'd lost but she was proud that someone in town had the guts to stand up. Heartened, I drove home at midnight on moonlit back roads. We'd fought the good fight. Maybe you could lose and still win. Ormond was still awake when I got back to the house. I took him to bed.

The next day Paradise seemed regained:

> Sat on the tailgate of Big Red, the red junker pickup O. bought for $500 and watched Ormond put up our TV antenna. I asked how he learned to do what he does, where he learned about the small clamps he was using to fasten the stay wires on the antenna. He said age eleven—he used to tour hardware stores for entertainment.
>
> The kids and I cleaned house, hauled trash, watered grass, and planted our first Christmas tree, a small Florida cypress. Anne attached two sponges to her feet with rubber bands and skated around the bathtubs to clean them. Ross dressed in red slacks, yellow t-shirt, a railroad engineer's hat, and strapped on a canteen "to go help his dad on the farm." Our pines, a year old, are up over the weeds, some three feet high. They look like green bottle brushes.
>
> Rich in love, rich in land.

I finished the second draft of *Organ Music* the following week and gave it to my dissertation co-directors, Jerry Stern and the novelist Janet Burroway. I started musing about writing another comic novel set in a town like Live Oak, located near Lake City, that also bans *Lysistrata* but for reasons reminiscent of the plot of the play, decides to reinstate it. I mentioned to

Susan Davis that I wanted to name the town Paradise and model the offended preacher, the superintendent, and the five school board members after the Seven Deadly Sins. She roared. "Oh, please make Sloth Roger Little."

On Tuesday, January 24, 1989, Ted Bundy was executed for the murder of the twelve-year-old Lake City girl, Kimberly Leach. A carnival atmosphere prevailed at the Florida State Prison at Starke. Crowds gathered with home-made posters and signs:

> THEODORE BUNDY
> YOUR SOME GUY
> GETTING YOUR KICKS
> WATCHING THEM DIE
> YOU'VE LIVED SO LONG
> DON'T KNOW WHY
> BUT TODAY'S THE DAY
> WE WATCH YOU FRY

Ray Callahan, who had invited Susan and Monya and me to move to San Francisco, told the *Lake City Reporter* he was in Starke "to welcome Ted Bundy into his next life."

After the execution, the Naked Lady Saloon in Lake City hosted "the Ted Bundy Barbecue," where, as County Commissioner Ron Williams put it, justice, along with free barbecued chicken, would finally be served.

On February 5, I copied a quote into my journal, another note to myself to live in the moment:

> If you're serious about shaking off your foreignness, Salad baba, then don't fall into some kind of rootless limbo instead. Okay? We're all here. We're right in front of you. You should really try and make an adult acquaintance with this place, this time. Try and embrace this city, as it is, not some childhood memory that makes you both nostalgic and sick. Draw it close. The actually existing place.

The author was Salmon Rushdie, a name then unfamiliar to me. Ten days later, sitting in the Grand Finale in Tallahassee with Janet Burroway, I learned that Iran had placed a $2.6 million bounty on Rushdie's head because his novel *The Satanic Verses* had offended the Ayatollah.

Once again I watched the widening circle of censorship, this time on an international scale. Bookstore owners around the world, even Sleepy Hollows like Tallahassee where no threats had been made, removed Rushdie's book from their shelves.

Initially, Rushdie was unrepentent. "Frankly, I wish I had written a more critical book," he said during an interview with BBC-TV. On February 18 he recanted:

> As author of *Satanic Verses* I recognize that Moslems in many parts of the world are genuinely distressed by the publication of my novel.
>
> I profoundly regret the distress that publication has occasioned to sincere followers of Islam.
>
> Living as we do in a world of many faiths this experience has served to remind us that we must all be conscious of the sensibilites of others.

The Ayatollah rejected the apology and exhorted Moslems around the world to "send him to hell." The bounty on Rushdie's head was raised to $5.2 million.

All this made our U.S. Court of Appeals' decision, which arrived at the height of the Rushdie ordeal, seem deeply ironic:

> The disputed materials have not been banned from the school. The humanities text and other adaptations of "Lysistrata" and "The Miller's Tale" are available in the school library. No student or teacher is prohibited from assigning or reading these works or discussing the themes contained therein in class or on school property.

How could three wise men be so naive? In the wake of the ban, no teacher in Columbia County would *consider* teaching these works. They wouldn't teach *less* controversial books; as one high school English teacher told Susan Davis, "I'd like to teach *To Kill A Mockingbird* but I know I don't dare." A middle school English teacher told us she's so tired of fundamentalist hassles she won't teach literature at all any more. "My students just do grammar," she said.

Censorship wasn't a single book banning; it was a contagion that spread with the fear that inevitably followed. I hoped, in the wake of the Rushdie ordeal, the Supreme Court would understand this.

By late February, it appeared we would never find out. The American Civil Liberties Union notified Sam that they were dropping our case:

> It is our perception that the possibility of a favorable decision by the U.S. Supreme Court is far outweighed by the likelihood of an unfavorable decision ... Unfortunately, the Supreme Court is not a consistently enlightened forum for resolution of cases such as this. In the event that the Supreme Court grants certiorari we will most certainly file an *amicus* brief in support of the plaintiffs' position.

Charles Willett, president of the Gainesville chapter of the A.C.L.U., called the next day. "Bad cases make bad law," he reminded me. He urged us not to continue the case. I told him I didn't know how we could with the A.C.L.U. out of the picture. He assured me I hadn't wasted my effort. "When you started this case you had no credentials on censorship issues. Now you do. You are not defeated," he said, "you are empowered."

On March 8, three years to the day after Ormond mentioned that a minister back in Lake City wanted the school board to ban the humanities textbook, Susan and I met with Sam Jacobson in his office on the twenty-ninth floor of the Independent Life Building in Jacksonville.

He sat at his desk in front of a bookshelf that held photographs of his wife and children, a small framed front page of the 1972 *New York Times* announcing his Supreme Court victory in the vagrancy case, and, not surprisingly, a series of books about Thomas Jefferson—*Jefferson the Virginian, Jefferson and the Rights of Man, Jefferson and the Ordeal of Liberty, Jefferson the President*. A dog-eared copy of Zinsser's *On Writing Well* lay face down on his desk amid a half-dozen accordion files and legal tablets, an hourglass, and a gold pen sticking out of a baseball-sized chunk of quartz.

Ansel Adams photos decorated the walls as well as a photo of Jacobson himself hunkered down on the side of a mountain.

Floor-to-ceiling windows overlooked the Dames Point, Mathews, Hart, and Main Street bridges spanning the St. Johns River. On a clear day, Sam told us, you could see all the way to Jacksonville Beach. Our view, however, was censored by great curved sheets of rain.

He said the decision had to be ours, but if we wanted to continue he would represent us *pro bono*. Susan and I said we hated to quit but we didn't want to do more damage than good by having the Supreme Court rule against us. Still, until someone asked the Court to limit *Hazelwood*, all censorship cases would stand in its shadow.

He agreed. The way he saw it, we only had a fifteen percent chance of being heard by this Supreme Court at all. If they denied our petition for a writ of *certiorari*, no real harm had been done; the 11th Circuit decision would stand, but without the national implications of a Supreme Court decision. If the Court granted *certiorari*, he believed we would get a fair hearing.

We decided to continue the case.

On April 5, in the same seminar room at Florida State where I had defended my doctoral exams a little more than three years before, I defended my dissertation and became if not the first, nonetheless, Dr. Johnson.

A week later Sam finished his petition to the U.S. Supreme Court, posing the judicial question once and for all: "Was A School Board Suppression of a Humanities Textbook Containing "Lysistrata" by Aristophanes and "The Miller's Tale" by Chaucer violative of the First Amendment?" He wrote, under Reason for Writ:

Guidance is needed from this Court as to the scope intended for *Hazelwood School District v. Kuhlmeier* (l988).

Both the Eleventh Circuit and the District Court expressed doubts about the School Board's judgment. But both courts felt prohibited by *Hazelwood* from intervening.

Petitioners believe that the Eleventh Circuit and District Court seriously misinterpreted and overapplied *Hazelwood*. Their interpretation of *Hazelwood* gives school boards almost absolute discretion in matters dealing with "potentially sensitive topics," including perceived vulgarity and sexuality, and leaves school boards virtually an unrestrained hand in the area of book bans based on claims of vulgarity and sexuality. The application given to *Hazelwood* below would leave even works universally acclaimed as great at the mercy of school board majorities finding them excessively vulgar or sexual, however puritanical and parochial the views of the board members.

The real truth is that the instant Board under purported justification of curriculum oversight was permitted to impose its own brand of religious and social orthodoxy—rooted in fundamentalist Christian precepts and valuing—upon the students of Columbia High and in turn upon all segments of the community.

. The judiciary cannot prudently cede to school boards the degree of First Amendment discretion which the lower courts here deemed mandated by *Hazelwood*. To do so would abandon literature and other instruments of learning invested with First Amendment attributes to the will, and perhaps whim, of school board majorities of the narrowest outlook. Judges are, and should be, the primary guardians of the Constitution. The First Amendment rights of high school students in literary matters cannot be abandoned to the degree of unfettered discretion by lay school board members allowed here.

This Court accordingly should issue its writ to correct the instant misapplication of *Hazelwood* and to preclude such misapplication hereafter.

He said it would be October at the earliest before we would know if the Supreme Court was willing to hear our case.

Thirteen.

We didn't hear from the high court that fall.

We did hear, that June, that the Corcoran Gallery had cancelled its exhibition of photographs by Robert Mapplethorpe, unleashing what came to be called the "Mapplethorpe mess" and spawning the Helms amendment that would threaten the reauthorization of the National Endowment for the Arts and force artists to sign a nonobscenity oath.

We did hear, that July, as we sat around our kitchen table overlooking the pond, that David Stevens was dead. Jimbo drove out to our house, one of the last David worked on, and told us the news. "When things slacked off here he took a job in Grand Caracas and fell from a scaffolding on a multilevel building," he said softly. David was thirty-five.

We did hear, in late August, that People for the American Way had published a new report citing seven Florida censorship cases, ours the most noted among them. In September, we read about the growing attack nationwide on books in school libraries. I called Dale Oaks, the librarian at Columbia High, and asked if any student had checked out the banned humanities textbook in the three years since the board placed it there.

"Not once," Dale said. He said the humanities course had been cancelled.

I called Jack Rankin, who had served on the school board's textbook committee and had since been appointed assistant principal. He told me the course had been cancelled in 1988. I asked him why. "Lack of interest," he said.

"Oh, come on, Mr. Rankin. Those classes were full."

"Well, it's been cancelled," he said. "Humanities is a dead duck in Columbia County."

In September, on my way to the Jacksonville airport, I stopped by Sam Jacobson's office. It was a glorious day; I could see all the way to Jacksonville Beach. I told him what Rankin had told me. "Well," Sam said, "the case may be moot, but that's for the Court to decide."

We didn't hear from the Court in November when the Suwannee Bulldogs won their third consecutive AAA state football title, tying the record number of wins.

We didn't hear the following spring, 1990, when the N.E.A. flap hit its height and Patrick Buchanan *et al.* campaigned for censorship in words reminiscent of the Reverend Fritz Fountain: "A nation absorbs its values through its art. A corrupt culture will produce a corrupt people, and vice versa; between rotten art, films, plays and books—and rotten behavior—the correlation is absolute."

We didn't hear from the Supreme Court the next fall when the Suwannee Bulldogs made state football history by winning their fourth consecutive AAA title.

From time to time during the year and a half since we decided to continue *Virgil et al.*, I would check with Sam Jacobson. Where was our case? What was the hold-up? He didn't know but he wasn't worried about the delay; the more time that passed between *Hazelwood* and the Court reviewing our own case, the better our chances of winning.

In March 1991, two years after Jacobson wrote his Petition for Writ of Certiorari, I heard from a reporter with the *Florida Times Union*. The Supreme Court had no record of our case on their computer, she told me. Did this mean we'd been denied *certiorari*?

I had no idea.

I called a clerk at the Supreme Court and, sure enough, they had no record of *Virgil et al*. She had no way of tracking it down without a case number. I didn't have one. I called Jacobson several times during the next six months, but he never called back.

On September 3, 1991, I wrote him a letter:

Dear Sam,

Susan and I need your help figuring out where we stand with the censorship case. I think we've gotten lost in some paperwork glitch.

I've phoned the Clerk's Office at the Supreme Court several times, and they have no record whatsoever of *Virgil et al.* The clerk asked for a case number, but I don't have a number written in my records.

If you have some information that would help us track this down, please let us know.

It was more important than ever to find out what had happened. Three days before, the last day of August, at an end-of-the-summer volleyball party at the Ceryak's house, sitting in the shade of a live oak, I heard someone mention that a born-again Christian, a man named Zeke Townsend, had crashed the last school board workshop to rave at the board and call them all sinners if they didn't censor *Of Mice and Men*.

I sat stunned for a moment. Out on the volleyball court, people were laughing and grunting. By the keg Ron Ceryak rigged in the back of his beat up blue pickup, others were talking about Townsend's complaint, making the same naive remarks I had heard in Lake City:

"They won't ban the book."

"Townsend's a crackpot."

"Tell him to take a look at the Bible … "

Cindy Swirko, the reporter who covered Suwannee County for the *Gainesville Sun*, shot me a grin. "So, did you know about this?"

"Hear about what?" I said, in denial.

"Zeke Townsend freaking out over Steinbeck. Calling it filth. Telling the school board to ban it."

Someone else laughed. "Oh, yeah, Blalock's got his shorts in a wad over this one." Charles Blalock was the superintendent.

"So," Cindy said, still grinning at me. "What are you going to do?"

"Nothing," I said.

"Oh, come on."

"Count me out."

When we drove home from the party, the *Suwannee Democrat* was there in our mail box. The story was on the front page:

> At Monday's school board workshop, a Dowling Park resident voiced his complaints over a summer reading list that had been assigned to his daughter.
>
> "Some of these books need burning instead of reading," said Zeke Townsend of Route 9, Box 960, Live Oak, whose daughter will be an eleventh grader at Suwannee high this year.
>
> Townsend became upset when his daughter showed him some of the pages of Steinbeck's *Of Mice and Men.* "It had a lot of cussing and vulgar talk in it," said Townsend. Townsend proposed that the school board take these books off the reading list and out of the schools.
>
> "I wore out a car taking my daughter to Westwood Christian School up there seven years two trips a day from Dowling Park to Live Oak, where she wouldn't be exposed to this. This ain't nothing but filth," Townsend said.

I handed Ormond the paper.

"Now remember," he said, trying to head off my rage, "the root word in fundamentalist is fun."

Thursday, September 4:

It's like a bad joke, the old one-two punch. It's life following fiction, the premise of my second novel—a town near Lake City banning books, too.

I move from one small town because they banned my two favorite works and now here in the next, it's starting again.

My first response was—not again! I'm not getting involved—then my conscience got me: if I don't fight censorship where I find it, what do I stand for? And the acid-test question I had for myself: would I have fought the case in Lake City if it had not been my 2 favorite works. The answer, I see now, is yes.

And I'm smarter now. Sadder but wiser. I've learned that the rational arguments—this is great literature; censorship is the work of totalitarian minds (didn't we just applaud Russia for quitting this kind of thing?); Bill of Rights/1st Amendment, etc.— have NO EFFECT WHATSOEVER ON BOOK BAN- NERS OR ON ELECTED OFFICIALS LIKE SUPER- INTENDENTS AND SCHOOL BOARDS.

I spoke with Barb Ceryak (who joined the school board last fall) for half an hour last night. I told her we have to pack a school board meeting—that's the only effective weapon we've got. We need to pack it quietly—feign complacency if we must—then storm the meeting—without letting the fundamentalists know. I feel like Bobby Bowden plotting a reverse, a punt rooskie (an interesting choice of words given the recent democratic upris- ing in Russia).

It's interesting, heartening, how Ormond's attitude is so different now—how his mind has changed about "going pub- lic" in the course of the last ugly battle. Now, too, he has a daughter in high school, 9th grade, who has the right to read but it might be taken away. She was in 3rd grade when the last battle started.

Jefferson's lesson: the price of liberty is eternal vigilance. Or eternal publicity, as the British novelist Tom Sharpe says in *Blott on the Landscape*.

This raises a fascinating judicial question—the U.S. Dis- trict Court and the U.S. Court of Appeals have ruled, in essence, that a person has no recourse in the courts against "the tyranny of board taste." If a board bans a book, that's a person's tough luck. Up the First Amendment. But what if that person leaves one small town because they ban books and moves to another only to find out they do, too? Wouldn't that show the courts that recourse in the courts was essential?

I told Anne last night while I tucked her in bed that now

she has a chance to fight censorship. She's getting the book from the school. "Zeke" still hasn't read it—par for the fundamentalist course—says he didn't finish it because he was put off by the language.

I told my sister about it. She said, "Why don't they ban mice?" I told my mother. She said, "Why don't they ban men?"

A note: Steinbeck is on the college prep reading list for senior honors English—students are required to read the books in the summer. Lynne Roy is the teacher; she's willing to offer alternative books. Barb says Lynne is tough; she won't back down; she's strong-minded and has been here forever.

It's hard to believe, sitting here at the table on my screened porch, mist on the meadow as tall as the pines, a hawk sailing across the bahia into the treeline, that a controversy is taking shape so nearby. The only conflict here is two herons squawking it out for territory down by the pond.

I've started jotting a list, people I'd seen at the volleyball game, people who might be willing to fight for the book. I came up with twenty. I felt my face getting hot as I did, that old fury rising: *how can the right to read depend on where you live?*

Here we go again.

I couldn't stay out; too much was at stake. The trouble was, I *liked* Live Oak. I wasn't in love with the town, but I'd fallen in love with the farm. I loved what we'd created, the house we'd built twice, the pines and bahia we'd planted, the habitat we'd created for threatened species—bluebirds, gopher turtles. I had worked too hard to be happy and I had succeeded, but I knew this would change if Live Oak censored books, too.

I had to do more than make lists.

I called Barb and asked her what the school board policy was for handling challenged books. She said it was the same as Lake City's—the offended party must file a formal complaint with the Superintendent who would appoint a review committee to examine the challenged material. The committee would make a recommendation to the board which would vote on the matter.

She said Zeke Townsend had still not filed a formal complaint, but Dr. Blalock wasn't going to wait. He'd asked Dr.

Tylk—the principal at Suwannee High—to appoint a committee to review *Of Mice and Men* and a second book Townsend raved to the school board about, Gordon Parks' novel, *The Learning Tree*.

I asked Barb if she thought I could join the committee?

She chuckled, knowing my past. "Well," she said, "I guess you could try."

I'd just finished reading an article about the Great Polluters infiltrating the Sierra Club, the Audubon Society, and the World Wildlife Fund. Two can play at this game, I thought.

I called Dr. Tylk and was able to say, as I hadn't been in Lake City, that our sons played on the same soccer team; we'd met at the Dairy Queen party at the end of the season. He remembered. I told him I taught English at Florida State and I was concerned about all this talk about censoring books.

Okay, okay, I didn't tell him I was one of the women who sued the school board in Lake City; the Great Polluters didn't show I.D.s either.

I asked if I could serve on the committee.

"No," he said, though he said it politely. "The board has strict guidelines for who can be on the committee, but it seems like a shame to me since parental involvement is the new educational buzzword."

I asked if I could come to the meeting, listen in, offer suggestions if anyone asked. He had no objection. The meeting was scheduled for 2:30 on Tuesday, September 10, at the school board building on Parshley Street behind Langford Field, home of the now famous Bulldogs.

I put down the phone and read Steinbeck's novel again, jotting down words as I went:

damn

God damn (that old chestnut)

bastard

Jesus Christ

son-of-a-bitch

The story seemed more topical than the first time I read it: George and Lenny were just like the homeless and unemployed holding signs on our interstate highways:

WILL WORK
FOR FOOD

I made notes about John Steinbeck's career. I called Sherry Millington, a friend who worked at the Suwannee River Regional Library, and asked if the library had a copy of Steinbeck's Nobel Prize citation. It didn't. I asked if I could add her name on my list of people willing to speak our for the book. She was more than willing. One of the librarians, Faye Roberts, said she was, too. I added their names to the list.

I was encouraged, too, that Blalock's grasp of the situation surpassed Silas Pittman's. He made an analogy in the paper: if parents don't want their child to watch a TV show, they can turn it off for their child, but not for all children.

Others in town had a different solution. On Friday evening, September 6, to culminate a week-long "uplifting revival" with the visiting Reverend Billy Mayo of Sunrise Ministries, the Westwood Baptist Church in Live Oak held a public book burning. The *Suwannee Democrat* ran the story and a picture of men, women, and children smiling as they dumped another barrel of books on the fire:

> The burning of the records, tobacco and books is to symbolize the beginning of a clean life free of anything that would hinder the soul from serving the only true God.
>
> "Mayo is doing a fantastic job for the youth of American today," said Sam Stapleton, congregation member. "The five nights Mayo was at Westside Baptist, we saw miracles you would not believe. We saw marriages restored, diseases healed and people saved. There was a good turnout every night ending with the bonfire as the grand finale. It is churches like Westside that will help assure that future generations will get the inspiration they need to lead a Godly and clean life."

My mother, who had feared for my life when I got involved in the censorship case in Lake City ("You'll end up like

Karen Silkwood!") wrote a letter to the editor pointing out the
irony of burning books when we'd just watched the Soviet
Union support free thought and democracy. She was the only
one who protested.

On Saturday afternoon, Tylk called back. Anne handed
me the phone with an astonished look on her face—why would
her principal be calling her *mother*? I'd been expecting the call.
I expected him to tell me he'd changed his mind and I couldn't
attend the review committee meeting.

Instead he said he'd been reviewing the school board
policy and it stated that "other qualified personnel" could sit on
the review committee. Blalock had agreed that "Miss Betty's
[Betty Castor] buzzword was 'accountability' which included
getting parents involved in key decisions. Without using my
name, he'd suggested to Blalock that perhaps they should
appoint a parent who thinks with the head and not just with the
heart. Blalock agreed.

"Why Dr. Tylk," I said, a little Blanche DuBois creeping
into my voice, "is this an invitation?"

He said, "Um, yes, it is."

I accepted. Tylk told me the meeting had been changed to
2 P.M., Thursday, September 12, at the high school library. I told
Ormond I would have to leave the meeting early to take Anne
to piano. He said, "Don't leave early. Stay at the meeting. I'll
take Anne to piano."

We met around a scarred wooden table in a small conference room at the high school library. Faye Roberts was also on
the committee. So were the three members of Suwannee High
School's English faculty, Annie Herring, Melissa Woodrum—
chair of the English department—and Lynne Roy, "the trouble-
maker," she called herself. She told us tales of past principals
barging into her classes and confiscating books that her students were reading. "At least this procedure is better than that,"
she assured us.

We discussed an "unwritten policy" that no high school
student could check out library books on the occult or write a
research paper on so-called Satanic subjects. The three teachers
agreed to challenge this later, and we turned from Satan to

Steinbeck.

When the A.C.L.U. dropped our case in February 1989, Charles Willett had told me, "You aren't defeated, you are empowered." If, in fact, I brought any power to the process in Live Oak, it was the language I'd learned as I pored over procedures, policies, and judicial decisions. We'd lost in the courts because *Hazelwood* said that a school board did not offend the First Amendment if it censored material for "legitimate pedagogical concerns."

There were other ways to apply pedagogy.

Once, on an A.C.L.U. panel in Gainesville, I had talked to the former Superintendent of Alachua County, James Longstreth. He told me how his county avoided censoring books. If a parent filed a complaint, the board simply compared the challenged book to the pedagogical goals set forth for that course. If they matched, that was that. The book stayed in the classroom. Alachua County hadn't banned books.

I acquainted the committee with James Longstreth's advice, and we compared the content of the two challenged novels to the pedagogical objectives for the class as set forth in "Policies for Selection of Instructional Materials." They were consistent, as we said in our letter to Dr. Tylk:

> The Committee unanimously agreed that both books are appropriate for the age level and subject of Honors English 3 at Suwannee High School. Further, both books are entirely consistent with the pedagogical objectives stated on page 1 of "Policies for Selection of Instructional Materials."
>
> The Committee strongly recommends that both books be returned to the classroom and to students immediately. We also recommend that the School Board re-examine and revise item 5 of "Policy on Challenged Materials in Suwannee County Schools": "Materials should not be removed immediately, but should be reviewed in light of the questions raised; however, materials should not be available for student use pending decision."

We found this statement to be contradictory and

believe that removing the material prior to review is an infringment of the other students' right to read.

I was well aware, as I left the meeting, that regardless of our recommendation, the school board could do whatever it pleased.

A few days later, Tylk acknowleged the letter and forwarded it to Dr. Blalock. Instead of going straight to the board, Blalock passed it on to the county-level Appellate Material Review Committee which met on Monday, October 7. Zeke Townsend did not come to the meeting, but Blalock distributed copies of his complaint, filed only against *Of Mice and Men*:

1. What brought this book to your attention?
    My daughter.
2. List your specific objections to the book.
    The cussing, vuglar [sic] talking and using the Lord's name in vain.
3. Quote offensive pasages and give page numbers.
    On back and seperate [sic] sheets of paper.
4. What was the theme of the book?
    I don't know, I didn't read it.
5. Have you read the entire book.
    No.
6. Have you read other titles by this author?
    No and I do not intend too either.
7. How did they compare with this book?
    If the words are as bad they should be banned from every library.
8. Do you know anything about the author's life?
    No. I do not want to know.
9. Did factors in his life influence this writing?
    I do not know anything about him only he is a vuglar [sic] talking man by what was found in the books.
10. What book in this field would you substitute for this one?
    Books with no cussing, vuglar [sic] talking, using the Lord's name in vain. Books for 11th graders decent and the people who decide what is read maybe they need to be checked out more closely.

NOTE: A committee of teachers, librarians, and qualified personnel will be appointed to evaluate the materials challenged and to make recommendations concerning it.

> *We do not know what you mean by qualified I presume that in somebody's decision they thought they had qualified people on the committee to pick these books out with all this vuglar, cussing and taking the Lord's name in vain in them I do not think so.*

Cheryl Chandler, a Live Oak parent completing a degree in library science at Florida State, read the "Freedom to Read" statement of the American Library Association:

> In a free society each individual is free to determine for himself what he wishes to read ... but no group has the right to take the law into its own hands and to impose its own concept of politics or morality upon other members of a democratic society. Freedom is no freedom if it is accorded only to the accepted and the inoffensive.

Melissa Woodrum read a statement from the faculty of the English Department. They recognized that the student body at Suwannee High was diverse. They did not want to interfere with parental authority. They would, in the future, allow for some choice on summer reading lists. But they also took seriously their job of preparing students for college: "It is important that advanced and college bound students read challenging material. The skills needed to read a Harlequin Romance, enjoyable though it is, are not comparable to those used reading Jane Austen's *Pride and Prejudice*."

Anne's ninth-grade English teacher, Suzie Tuttle—a firecracker with a mane of red hair—strode to the mike and explained that Steinbeck used language to realistically portray the characters in the book. "The theme is the sacrifice of pure love between two men ... if children are not exposed to the theme of sacrifice and love then I think that they are missing out on an important theme of life."

I made a brief statement that a school system puts its students at a disadvantage when it bans the books they should read. I quoted Chris Vedova, a student at Columbia High when the board banned "The Miller's Tale" and *Lysistrata*. He supported the banning, but when he went to college and read the two classics, he wrote a letter to the *Lake City Reporter*:

> After studying both works, I see no reason why they were banned, and actual outrage at the action of the School Board ... I now realize, and wish I had earlier, that censorship in any form cannot be tolerated in a free society. The only way that our youth can develop into responsible adults is through responsible education.

The Appellate Committee unanimously recommended reinstating *Of Mice and Men* and offering choice on reading lists in the future. Mary Daniels, an English teacher from Branford, summed up their thinking: "Students are citizens, too. They deserve the same rights." She had done what we'd hoped the U.S. Appeals Court would do—sweep aside *Hazelwood* and returning to the thinking of *Tinker*: "It can hardly be argued that either students or teachers shed their constitutional rights to freedom of speech or expression at the schoolhouse gate."

Blalock sent the recommendation to the board which would make its decision on Thursday, October 17. While I waited to see if another school board would ban another great book because of bad language, I listened to the Senate Judiciary Committee cross examine Anita Hill about Long Dong Silver and pubic hair.

On October 16, the day before the big meeting, a letter from Zeke Townsend appeared in the *Suwannee Democrat*:

> I didn't want to read this book "Of Mice and Men" by John Steinbeck because of all the bad language but I had to where I would know what I was talking about. When I finished it I asked God to forgive me for reading such trash.
>
> I also disagree with Mrs. Susie Tuttle, a high school English teacher. She said it was pure love

between these two men. Now if it was why, did George cuss Lennie for all those bad cuss words all through the book. If he loved him so much, explain to me why he put a gun to his head and killed him ...

Miss Roy, I would like to know how you are going to grade them? Is it which man could cuss the most or the biggest? Also I would like to know if you cuss like John Steinbeck does in these books? Would you use this language in your Sunday school class or at a public gathering? Do you read these books out loud in class and do you require the students to cuss a little for you? Thisis the kind of language that peole use around a juke joint ...

These books, with all of the filthy language, was an insult to the Christian people. I resnt it to the highest degree.

I carried my daughter to Westwood Christian School for seven years and was well pleased. I didn't have to worry about what they were teaching my child because I knew what they stood for. That is why I trusted them. I thank God for those kind of people, they are doing a good job by our children.

To the two committees that met at the high school and at the superintendent's office which are: Miss Lynne Roy, Mrs. Annie Herring, Mrs. Mellisa Woodrum, Mrs. Faye Roberts, and Mrs. Claudia Johnson. Also Mrs. Margie Miller, Mr. Jessie Philpot, Mrs. Mary Daniels, Mr. Marvin Johns, Mrs. Eveline Durhart and Mr. Charles Blalock. You have already let the people of Suwannee County know that you approve of these vulgar books by voting to return them to the shelf and to our classrooms.

I think we need to expose these people to every church congregation in Suwannee County and to every newspaper in he state.

To the school board members and the superintendent, you are in a position of authority to do something about this at your next school board meeting and if you choose not to take these vulgar talking books out of the school system, well then don't waste your money to run for reelection.

He called the school board office and asked who I was. The two secretaries, Liz Paulk and Ann Doswell, were both friends of mine—I'd known Ann for years and Liz was the mother of one of Ross's best friends. They knew what I'd done in Lake City, but they glanced at each other and said, "She's a college professor."

Liz Paulk told me about Townsend's call the next morning, the day of the meeting, when I dropped Ross at school. I asked if she knew how the school board would vote. She didn't. No one did. We knew Barb was opposed to book banning, but there were four others: Jessie Philpot, director of the Food Stamp program for Suwannee and Hamilton counties; Sam Barnett, a former car dealer, now semi-retired; J. M. Holtzclaw, a farmer; and Bill Howard, the office manager at Musgrove Construction. They just weren't talking. Liz didn't think they'd ban books, but then, Ed Montgomery had said the same thing back in Lake City.

For the rest of the day, I worked on the statement I'd make that night to the board. I wanted to stick to practical matters, information I thought a school board could *hear*: educational budgets were shrinking. These copies of Steinbeck were paid for. It was fiscally foolish to chuck them out.

Universities were cutting back, too, making it harder for high school students to get in. The better read would have a far better chance of being admitted. I called John Barnhill, the head of Admissions at Florida State, and armed myself with quotes and statistics.

And, most importantly, everyone who claimed concern about education (except, perhaps, for President Bush) was trying to restore academic excellence to our schools. No school board could achieve this by banning great books.

I took a break to glance at *They Shoot Writers, Don't They?*, a collection of essays about censorship, one written by Rushdie before he published *Satanic Verses*. There is, near the front of the book, a cartoon of a tree bearing names of great writers—Dante,

Shakespeare, Chaucer, and others. At the base of the tree stands a man with an axe.

He is chopping.

Virgil does not appear on the tree, but I realized he might. No writer, it seemed, was safe from the censors. Recently they had banned *My Friend Flicka* because of bad language and *Little Red Riding Hood* because the child carries wine in her basket. *The Aeneid* would clearly be trouble: Aeneas tarries with Dido at Carthage; when he abandons her to continue his travels, she throws herself on a fire. What might this teach our children? Burn in a pyre?

What had begun as court nomenclature took on new meaning: the tree, I realized, was Virgil *et al.*

Fourteen.

The meeting that night was unlike any I'd seen in Lake City. Both sides were well represented, divided by an aisle up the middle. Zeke Townsend—a grim-looking man with a sandy red flat-top—sat in the front row next to his daughter in front of fifty or more of his faithful. Steinbeck's supporters crowded into the opposite side. I sat between Ross and Ormond who sat next to Anne, their first censorship meeting. Lynne Roy and Melissa Woodrum sat behind us, their statements in hand. Sherry Millington sat in front, along with Faye Roberts, Annie Herring, and other librarians and teachers in town.

Before us, beneath a row of portraits of Suwannee County's past superintendents, the board sat at three tables arranged in a U. On our left, Barb Ceryak sat by Bill Howard; on our right, Sam Barnett sat by board attorney, Victor Africano; in the middle, J. M. Holtzclaw and Charles Blalock flanked the chairman, Jessie Philpot. A microphone had been placed in the center facing the board.

By seven o'clock all seats were taken. Those who couldn't find seats leaned on the wall in the back. Marvin Johns, the assistant superintendent, opened the meeting with a passage from Psalms. We all stood for the Pledge of Allegiance. When we were seated again, Blalock reviewed the board's policy for challenged materials. He noted that Mr. Townsend had not filed a formal complaint against *The Learning Tree*, so the discussion would center only on Steinbeck. He read the Review and Appellate committee's recommendations to return *Of Mice and Men* to the library and to "desirous" students in honors English;

an alternative book would be offered to "non-desirous" students.

"At this time," he said, "Mr. Townsend is here, and I think we should hear from those who support Mr. Townsend's side at this time."

Zeke Townsend walked to the mike. He turned it so he could speak to the crowd. He held up a copy of Steinbeck. "I'm here again tonight to talk about these books. I'm not opposed to the book itself, what I'm against is the way it's written, the language. Now the Bible tells us not to take the Lord's name in vain—"

Across the aisle, someone shouted, "Amen!"

Our side turned, wide-eyed. Anne and Ross were astonished. They had never seen a revival. They had never heard a crowd shouting back.

"Now these books have the Lord's name in vain," Townsend said. "They've got some of the worst cussing in 'em, *Of Mice and Men*, *The Learning Tree* by Gordon Parks."

"Amen!"

Anne and Ross giggled, not so much from disrespect but the shock of it all. I whispered to both, "It doesn't reflect well on you or on me if you laugh at these people." They straightened their faces.

"Now I'm against this filthy talk," Townsend said. "We go to church, we teach our child right on Sunday morning for a couple hours, we send them to school five days a week, and they put trash in their minds."

"Amen!"

Zeke narrowed his eyes at Lynne Roy. "If you put that garbage in his mind, if he don't never accept God as his savior, he dies and goes to hell, well then it's the teacher what taught him—the blood of that child'll be on that teacher."

"Amen!"

Sherry Millington turned around and whispered to me, "He's not talking about the book, he's *preaching*."

I nodded.

"Now I'm opposed to this," Townsend shouted. "It's wrong. Everybody here knows it's wrong. You go to church, all these people go to church, God gave you eyes, you know it's wrong, I don't have to get up here and tell you it's wrong, you *know* it's wrong."

"Right! Amen!"

He ranted about the country going downhill. "God has blessed our country, but we haven't blessed him back as a whole."

"You're right."

"I believe in doing what's right. I believe in standing up for what's right no matter what people say. Sticks and stones may break my bones but words will never hurt me."

"Amen!"

"If I had any doubts that I was just a little bit wrong I wouldn't be here tonight but I know I'm right and I'm gonna stand up."

"Amen!"

"We say we love America. I love America. I love my community. I do. I love this county, and this state. And the Bible says I got to love all of y'all or go to hell. But y'all got some ways I don't like. I tell you, I don't like 'em. God didn't say I had to love your ways, he said that I had to love you. I love every one of you, but you got some ways I don't like."

He testified about being sick years ago, losing weight. His doctors told him to make out his will. He went for a drive to decide which of his farms to leave to his daughter. "I'm on my knees in that field out there about an hour before sundown. I promised the Lord if he healed me, that I'd live for Him the rest of my life. God healed me in that field out there, I gained fifty-two pounds back, I gained fourteen years. God give me fourteen. I'm looking for fifteen, but whatever time I got left on this earth, I'm gonna live for the Lord. And I'm gonna stand up for his teachings."

"Amen!"

He waved his copy of Steinbeck. "Now we know this is wrong."

"Yeah, that's right!"

"We *know* that's wrong."

"Amen!"

"Ain't nobody got to *tell* us it's wrong." He was picking up speed, getting louder and louder. His side of the room was clapping and shouting. Anne and Ross sat, their faces a mix of fascination and fright. I felt a little frightened myself.

"When you use profanity like's in these books, using the Lord's name in vain, and all that unnecessary cussing, that's wrong."

"Yeah, he's right!"

"You can get your point over to somebody without cussing. I can talk to anybody anyhow without cussing. And I think we need to take these cussing books out of the school system. We're messing up these children's minds."

"Right! Amen!"

"We ain't livin' for the Devil, we livin' for the Lord."

"Amen!"

"When somebody gets sick, he asks the Lord to heal him."

"Amen!"

Townsend dropped to his knees and bent his head toward the floor. "When somebody gets sick, you don't say, 'Devil, I want you to heal me, Devil.'"

His side laughed and applauded.

"You need to get on your knees and ask God to heal you!" Townsend threw his arms open toward heaven. "'Cause *He's* the only one can heal you."

"Amen!"

"Ain't no man in this country or no other country got the power to heal no man."

"Amen!"

"But God heals his people. Now you get healed, God does it. Ain't no *man* do it 'cause he can't. *God* heals people."

"Amen!"

Jessie Philpot cut Townsend off. "Thank you for your presentation. We don't want to use all the time. These others would like to speak."

Townsend stood up. "I know, but y'all gave me good money." His side chuckled. He dusted his knees and said to the crowd, "I thank you for coming."

"We thank you, Mr. Townsend," Philpot said.

Several others condemned the book, including one of the two Presbyterian ministers in town, Jim Walkup, who praised Townsend's "diligence in checking out his daughter's reading material. We need more parents like him."

"Yeah. Amen."

"The reason that pornography, profanity, and violence have so pervaded our society is that we have remained silent too long."

"That's right."

"Mainly because we fear the wrath of liberals who mistake freedom for rights."

"Uh huh."

"Fundamentalists, of which I'm proud to be one, have been painted as a minority seeking to impose their values on everyone else."

"Yeah."

"The real minority consists of the liberals who pretend to speak for the majority. We find them in the National Education Association, the National Organization of Women, the National Endowment for the Arts, the American Civil Liberties Union, the majority of the media, and the left wing of the Democratic party."

"In the name of Jesus!" someone shouted.

He quoted Goebbels, Adolph Hitler's Minister of Propaganda, "Let me control the books and I will control the country."

"He's right. Uh huh."

"And the liberals have controlled the books for too many years now and you see how our morals and ethics have degenerated." He quoted Blalock, "I think John Steinbeck is a literary giant. Like all great writers he has to portray lifelike characters in their own jargon."

Someone on our side shouted, "Amen!"

"Steinbeck is a literary giant," Walkup continued.

"Amen!" we all shouted.

"He won the Pulitzer Prize in 1940 for *The Grapes of Wrath*."

"Yeah, uh huh," we said.

"But Steinbeck is a *filthy-mouthed* literary giant."

The other side laughed. Some applauded.

"Since when has it been necessary to portray lifelike characters in their own jargon?"

"Never!"

Reverend Walkup relegated *Of Mice and Men* to the "garbage dump" and walked back to his seat amid wild applause.

Jessie Philpot asked speakers to limit their presentations to two minutes.

Doyle Glass, the minister at Zeke Townsend's church, the Dowling Park Church of God, walked to the mike and warned the audience, "I think there's probably more books than just the ones that's listed there tonight that we're talking about, and personally, I'd like to see them every one removed and taken out of the schools."

"Amen!"

When Glass was finished, a bearded heavy-set man, Curtis Rice, ambled up to the mike. "I don't speak as well as a lot of people do, I don't pastor no church, I lived through the hell of what ya'll tried raising kids up to go through, but by the grace of God I got out of it about thirteen years ago."

"Amen!"

"Look around the world today. I saw twenty-three people was killed last night in Texas. I saw there was a twenty-two year old girl starting out life today was killed. Somebody hit her automobile. I see kids fifteen years old, pregnant and having babies. I see the whole world falling apart. These people out here—"he gestured to us—"do like you want to, I don't come to your house, I don't knock on your door, I don't force you to do what you don't want to do, so don't force the Devil on me or my young'uns."

"Uh huh, he's right."

"When Brother Zeke Townsend called me on the telephone and he read that word, he said them words he shocked me so bad I like to died. I hung up the phone and went in the bathroom and me and my wife prayed because that man said them words that was in that book, just reading them, and then y'all give them to children fifteen, sixteen, seventeen years old, take the Bible away, they can't read the word of God—"

"Right."

"They can't pray."

"Right."

"It's against the law to pray."

"Right."

"It's against the law to read the Bible."

"Right!"

"But prayer works."

"Yes, it does!"

"I think we should go back to praying."

"Amen!"

His staccato rhythm had worked up his half of the crowd. They were clapping and shouting. By comparison, the meetings back in Lake City had been soporific, and that board had been swayed. I tried to gauge our board's reaction, but they sat there stone-faced, inscrutable.

"You say it's okay to talk like that," Rice said to our side. "You say this is love. Well, love is what Jesus Christ gave his life so we would not have to die and go to hell, love is what David had for Saul, that he loved him so much he would not go against him, that's love, good love, you want to serve the Devil, I'm not gonna stop you, but show hell to my child—"

A woman's voice interrupted. "Am I in a church or a school board meeting?" Suzie Tuttle stood in the aisle, arms akimbo.

"We's in church right now," Townsend said. His side chuckled.

Suzie sat down in the chair Curtis Rice had vacated. Jessie Philpot seized the silence and thanked Rice for speaking. "Anyone who would like to speak in favor of the book can come forward now."

Melissa Woodrum walked toward the mike as Curtis Rice walked back to his chair. Suzie Tuttle realized she was in it. She started to stand.

"No, now, you take it," Rice said. "I've given better things to the Devil."

Melissa Woodrum turned the mike back toward the board and started to read the statement she'd read to the Appellate Committee. A few people heckled.

I said, "Let her speak! She listened to you!" Anne and Ross stared, amazed, at their mother. Ormond squeezed my hand— *take it easy*. Melissa finished the statement without interruption.

A senior, Julie Farlas, spoke next, a rushed soft-spoken plea for the freedom to read. When she sat down, Suzie Tuttle strode to the mike, long hair swaying. She put her hand on the mike and said to the board, "Could I turn this around? I feel like I'm pointed in the wrong direction." The board members nodded. She turned the mike toward the room full of people. She smiled. "I must say that this is the most exciting meeting I've ever attended. Really. And I've *never* been called the Devil until tonight."

"I didn't call you the Devil," Curtis Rice said from the back of the room. "I just said I give up more, better things than that to the Devil."

Suzie smiled. "Okay, I just wanted to clarify that."

"Okay," Rice said.

Friendly laughter.

Suzie said she wasn't there as a teacher, she was there as a parent, as a representative of her children and their right to read. She acknowledged that other parents had different ideas about what was best for their children. "When someone encroaches on that territory, it can bring about fighting words. Just like we've heard here tonight. And we don't need to fight, y'all. We don't need to fight. We are a community. And I see a dividing line here." She gestured toward the aisle. "I don't like to see that."

She told the story of her old sow, how, when she'd encroached on her babies, "she took me and tossed me across that old stile." She said she now realized that the schools may have "disappointed or misled our students' parents into believing that we are trespassing on their rights as parents, and certainly none of us ever intended to do that." She spoke so sincerely, no one else seemed to notice she'd compared fundamentalist parents and pigs.

She addressed Townsend directly, reminding him they'd been friends, fellow farmers, for years, and that they had been through a similar matter four years before when Jennifer was in the ninth grade and he was offended by the language in *When the Legends Die*. "I'm truly sorry that instead of approaching Miss Roy or the administration regarding this matter before you came before the school board. You didn't give us the opportunity to reassure you that we as both teachers and parents are on your side. We are on your side regarding the choices that you make for your daughter. As a personal acquaintance of your family I know that you know that we all want what's best for our daughters."

Townsend's side shifted, uneasy. Her appeal to Townsend and their common past had disarmed them. It had the emotional force of Scout in front of the lynch mob in that often banned book, *To Kill a Mockingbird*: "Don't you remember me, Mr. Cunningham? I'm Jean Louise Finch. You brought us some hickory nuts one time, remember?"

"I want my daughter to read *Of Mice and Men*," Suzie continued directly to Townsend. "I want my daughter be able to experience the freedom of choice. I see you shaking your head. We disagree on this, but on other matters you and I have a great deal of respect for each other."

"We do," said Zeke Townsend.

"We do," Suzie said. "We respect each other for what we stand for. We may disagree on this matter but we do agree on others. And we agree that I care a lot for your daughter. You know that. I would never put your daughter in a position where she gets hurt. If you did not want her to read this book, I assure you we would never have had her read this book. Anyway, we're the same and we are different, but we can coincide if we both respect each other for what we believe and what is best for all our children. And believe me, the respect of parents is what we're all about at Suwannee High School. We have clarified our departmental requirements, we have clarified and encouraged parent participation. We want you to read the books before we give them to the kids. We did not intend to slight you. I am speaking from my heart, not from a piece of paper. But I hope that you'll remember one thing. What others prefer for their children may not be what I prefer for mine. And I request, I request, that the school board maintain the freedom of parents to choose by reinstating *Of Mice and Men* and *The Learning Tree* to the library and to the reading list with the stipulation that parents are allowed to read the books first, parents are allowed to select what they want for their children to read, parents are allowed to *recommend* books for their students to read, and thereby provide avenues of choice for all of us. Thank you very much for your time."

Both sides applauded as she sat down. Jessie Philpot

asked if there were others who wanted to speak for the book.

Faye Roberts made a brief statement, also as a parent. Like Suzie Tuttle, she wanted her children to read *Of Mice and Men* and other controversial books and deal with "all kinds of ideas."

When she was finished Jessie Philpot tried closing the hearing, "All right, I think we have heard from those opposed to the book and those in favor of the book."

"Go on," Ormond said, nudging me. "You're missing your chance."

I turned to Lynne Roy. "What about you?"

"You go on," she said.

I stood up, a little faint-hearted, and walked to the mike, my six typewritten pages in hand. I smiled sheepishly at the board. "Um, mine's kind of long."

"Can you make it shorter?" Jessie Philpot asked politely.

I nodded, flipping the pages, editing my speech on the spot. I kept it simple: budgets were shrinking; these books were paid for. Several board members nodded and smiled. I'd finally found common ground.

I repeated what Florida State's director of admissions had told me: he gets between twelve and thirteen thousand applications a year for three thousand places for freshmen. The law of supply and demand is driving the standards up further. The minimum SAT score was already up to 1000, for ACT, 24. Half of the questions on these entrance exams tested verbal skills, reading comprehension, and critical thinking. I noticed Barb wrote this down.

"All these skills are enhanced by giving our students more challenging reading in high school. I asked Mr. Barnhill how important it was for students to read widely in high school, to be exposed to a range of challenging literature. He said, 'I work a lot with national merit students, the ones who do the best on the SAT, and, invariably, these are students who have read a lot of books, students whose parents have read to them when they were little, people who have a real interest in reading. These are people who have read the great books.' I asked him if this included *Of Mice and Men*. He said he was sure the better students had read it."

I quoted Ann Durham, the Academic Coordinator for the

English Department at Florida State: "The emphasis is shifting from writing about literature to examining controversial issues in literature. In high school, if they are told how to think and what to think, when they get to college and a teacher says, 'What do you think?', they'll be lost. College is hard enough now without crippling students in high school."

Out of time, I cut to my punch line. "If Mr. Townsend wants to cripple his children, that is his choice. He has no right to cripple mine." I thanked the board and walked back to my seat, past Zeke Townsend staring slit-eyed at me. Anne and Ross and Ormond patted my back as I sat.

"That's my momma!" Anne crowed.

"*Hush*," I said, smiling. No matter how the vote went, at least my children had witnessed this meeting.

Lynne Roy spoke last. She answered the questions Zeke Townsend had asked in the paper the previous day. "I found them so ludicrous that I wanted to facetiously respond, 'Yes, Mr. Townsend, we line up all the obscenities on one side of the page and their definitions on the other side, and we match them together.' If we ever gave a test such as this, it may surprise Mr. Townsend that all of the students would make a hundred on the test."

Our side chuckled.

"Not all students may use these words, but if they have walked the halls of Suwannee High School, if they have read a contemporary novel, then they have not only heard the words, they have read them in their own choice of reading material. I do not believe that reading *Of Mice and Men* is their first exposure to these words."

She went on to defend her reading list, the books she'd selected, including *Of Mice and Men*. She cited a list of sixty books that have been challenged, banned, burned in the United States in the last fifteen years for reasons ranging from "inappropriate language" to "promoting a depressing or negative view of life." She read some of the names: "Arthur Miller, Ernest Hemingway, John Steinbeck, J. D. Salinger, Kurt Vonnegut, Alice Walker, Mark Twain, Anne Frank, Ray Bradbury, Harper Lee, Harriett Beecher Stowe, Maya Angelou, Joseph Heller, and C. S. Lewis."

I thought of the cartoon of the tree.

"These are some of our finest American authors," Lynn continued. "William Shakespeare and Rudyard Kipling are also included. You may recognize some of your favorite authors. If you have children, you may very well have read them a banned book. Also included on this list: three of Shel Silverstein's books—*Where the Sidewalk Ends, Light in the Attic,* and *The Giving Tree*—*Where's Waldo*—yes, one of the most popular children's characters of today; *Garfield: His Nine Lives;* and *Charlie and the Chocolate Factory* by Roald Dahl—banned because it is considered 'to espouse a poor philosophy of life.' One of the most frightening examples of banning is that of *The Living Bible.* Not only was this Bible banned in Gastonia, North Carolina, it was burned because it was considered 'dangerous' and 'a perverted commentary on the King James Version.'"

She closed by recounting a grisly story of gang rape, mutilation, revenge, then informed the board and the crowd that it was straight out of Chapter 19 of the Book of Judges in the King James version of the Bible. "Do we ban the entire Bible because of this story?" Lynne asked the board. "No, we don't. We accept it as part of the greater work of the word of God. Focusing on one part of a literary work and condemning the entire literary work is the most dangerous aspect of censorship. We need to take a stand now and let people know that we have confidence in their ability to choose what is right for them."

Our side exploded with shouts and applause. A few people shouted, "Amen!"

Jessie Philpot tried to close the discussion, but Townsend broke in. He wanted to speak one more time.

Philpot sighed. "I'll let you, but please be very brief because if you continue here, we'll be here a long long time."

Townsend walked back to the mike. He told Suzie he had a lot of respect for her, that he loved her. He turned to Blalock. "I just want to know what would happen if a student used language like this in school. "Would y'all suspend him?"

Blalock acknowledged that school board policy prohibits use of profane language in the school on the part of students or instructional personnel.

"But it's okay to read it," said Townsend. There was a

pause, then I heard my name.

"This lady who just got up, this Claudia Johnson, didn't she file a lawsuit against the Columbia County school board?"

It was chilling to be singled out, to become Zeke Townsend's target. Why now, at the end of such an emotional meeting? Still, I was proud of what I'd done in Lake City.

"Yes, I did," I replied. "I fight censorship whenever I find it in my home town."

People around me applauded.

Townsend looked at some notes he was holding, "Let me see, May 12, 1986, that's when she sued the board ... ."

I realized what he was up to, that old strategy Orin Hatch and his cronies had just used so successfully to undermine the serious charges Anita Hill brought against Clarence Thomas— discredit the woman. Well, Townsend wasn't going to do it to me. I rose like a flame—white-hot, my eyes flashing. Blalock's eyes widened as I stood up and shouted at Townsend. "My life and my actions are not the issue here tonight. Leave me out of it!"

"Right! Amen!" I heard a few people say.

Jessie Philpot warned Townsend to stick to the issue or he would have to ask him to sit. Townsend persisted, "What I want to know is how Suwannee High School could pick her to be on the committee when she's already in a lawsuit in Columbia County—"

Sherry Millington must have realized what I had because she cried out, *"This is a personal attack on this woman and I want it to stop!"*

A startled silence. "All right," Townsend said. He walked back to his seat.

There was a pause, then Jessie Philpot calmly spoke to the board. "Okay, you've heard both sides. Now we'd like to hear from the board. Does anyone on the board have anything they would like to say?"

Barb spoke first. "I want to thank everyone who came here tonight for their interest in education. I have to say that I'm opposed to banning books in the community and yet I also think we have an obligation to parents who are concerned about their children's education and there obviously are many parents here who are. I'm very pleased by the statement that was read by the English Department because it seems to me that they expressed a willingness to try to find something that worked for as many people as possible and I think their statement that they're willing to put choice on their lists so that no child would be required to read a book that would be offensive to them, it seems to me that that should somewhat alleviate the problem."

Philpot asked the other board members if they wanted to speak. No one responded. He thanked us for coming, then he said, "I concur with Mrs. Ceryak. I certainly don't think that we should go around banning whole books in our school system. I certainly think the English Department has extended themselves to the point where they're willing to go out of their way and allow each individual who objects to reading these books other books that would be accommodating to them. I certainly think that that shows they're making a good faith effort not to offend any parent that objects to these books that other parents may want their children to read. And I think when we start banning books we also need to take into consideration that the material that I may object to may be okay with someone else. It may offend me but we can't infringe on someone else's right to have that choice to read. I think we all need to remember that and I'm very concerned about each of you that oppose the material; I too would not want my child to be exposed to that kind of profanity, but each of us sitting here tonight knows that in many workplaces this is very common whether we want to admit it or not, it's very common, and certainly our children need to be made aware of what to expect beyond high school. They need to be prepared for it. I do not endorse it and I'm not telling you that I endorse it but I'm telling you that it's a reality in our society, and I personally would not like to see it split the community that we all live in and I'm willing to work to make this a better place to live."

"That's two," I whispered to Ormond. We needed one more to win.

Bill Howard leaned toward the mike. "My position is I think, I feel like, I'm just as big, as much a Christian as anybody in this room. I feel like we are charged with the responsibility to serve every child in our schools. And I'm not professing that every child's a Christian or his parents are Christian. I feel obligated that we have to serve his family whether they want their children— And I feel like there are a lot of children who probably would have not even known this book or paid much attention but every child now is going to stand in line waiting to read it, I guarantee you, I got three children and I know."

Knowing laughter.

"But what I'm saying is I think we're charged with our responsibility to give every child the best responsibility we possibly can, and if it takes this kind of literature to do it and the parents are willing to do it, I feel like that we have to provide that for them. I don't like my child using expressions like this, we don't talk like that in my house, but I know that that's part of it, and if I thought that my voting against it would keep her from being subjected to it, I would vote against it but I know that they're subjected to it in the hallways, on the playground, and the football field, and the band room and every aspect of education, our children are subjected to it, and I don't want anyone to go away from here tonight thinking that I'm promoting it because I'm not but I really feel like this—if Marjorie Miller's daughter or child wanted to read that and Marjorie was in favor of it, they should have that right. I believe the Constitution allows that. And I think that we would be hurting them if we did not provide that. I do however feel that if there is a parent who objects to any book, I don't care if it's Tom and Jerry, I believe there should be different books for them, but I feel like that we have to provide the best possible education for the kids. If that means making books available to those that want to read it, and their parents agree, I think we should let them."

I looked at Ormond. "That's three. They're not going to ban it."

Sam Barnett took it from there. "I have real mixed emotions about the book. My child did not read it when he was in the honors program, he chose not to read it, we backed that, but we are charged with the responsibility of having an open society and there are many many TV programs on that we do not watch. We go to very very few movies because of the language and the violence but as Bill has stated, if we could, if this board here tonight could say that we—by our vote here tonight—that we would discontinue all that, we probably would have five people voting to do just exactly that. But unfortunately we do have to live in a diverse society and we do have to abide by the Constitution of the United States, and I think if we do start banning books then we are going to invite further division in the community and invite further lawsuits which as we all know are very very costly and in the end the Supreme Court is going to say that you don't have the right to ban books."

I felt like raising my hand, "Oh, sir, no, you're wrong," but I kept my mouth shut.

"So then what we're going to do is turn around and spend a lot of money that could go into the classroom for other things and unfortunately that's what we're faced with, and if I felt like that one vote would change that, I would certainly stand up and say I'm going to vote against it and hope that that would change the way that people talk and the way people live, but I'm afraid that that isn't going to happen."

J. M. Holtzclaw spoke last. "Like Mr. Howard said, I'm a Christian myself. I try to live by the Bible. The Bible is my Lord and the Bible charges me with obeying the law of the land. The law of the land is the Constitution. At this point the Constitution has been interpreted to mean that we have the right to speak and read and we have that freedom. I'm opposed to banning books. I'm opposed to profanity in the book but I'm opposed to banning books, and as long as you have that choice and I have the choice of whether my child reads that book or does not read it, and as I understand it, you have that choice, and I have that choice of allowing or not allowing my child to read this book, and on that basis I'm opposed to banning this book."

There was a silence.

"It's unanimous," I whispered to Anne, Ross, and Ormond. Five and a half years before, it had been a unanimous vote to ban the humanities textbook.

Our side burst into applause.

Blalock stood and spoke with renewed energy, fueled, I think, by relief. "Okay, I would like to restate my recommendation for the board at this particular time which would be the unanimous recommendation that was made by the two committees. I have a copy of cases that have been before the

Supreme Court and deal with the First Amendment to the Constitution—freedom of speech and freedom of the press, and each time that each case has been taken before the Supreme Court it has been a futile effort."

Ormond and I exchanged glances. Hadn't he heard of *Hazelwood v. Kuhlmeier*? Hadn't he heard that we'd lost in *Virgil et al.*? He didn't know or he chose to ignore it. Either way, I was grateful.

Blalock reminded the audience that he and the board had the responsibility to educate all of the children who came to them, "the responsibility of helping them realize their potential so that they will become productive citizens in the country."

Barb moved to approve the recommendation. Bill Howard seconded. The vote was, in fact, unanimous.

Jessie Philpot thanked everyone for coming and expressing their interest, then he asked for a brief recess.

I congratulated Lynne Roy and Melissa Woodrum and Suzie Tuttle and thanked Sherry Millington for making Townsend sit down. Later, Blalock thanked her as well. Even later, Victor Africano said to school board secretary, Ann Doswell, "Did you see the way Townsend fell to his knees and threw open his arms? I thought he was going to start singing 'Mammy'!"

I didn't hear any of this, until later. After thanking the teachers and Sherry, we headed out of the building. I threw my head back and shouted, "Praise Jesus!" I meant it. For this night at least, God, whatever one perceived Him/Her to be, was in favor of the freedom to read.

We got in the car.

"Unanimous," I exclaimed, still amazed, overjoyed. "The teachers," I said, "made the difference. If they'd protested back in Lake City, the board might not have done what it did."

"Oh, I don't know," Ormond said, heading home. "The ghost of *Virgil et al.* was in the board room tonight." I savored the thought. Maybe we'd done some good after all.

When we got back to the farm, Anne and Ross jumped out of the car and ran toward the house. Ormond and I walked slowly behind, holding hands, enjoying the moment, the triumph, the cold starry night, the Milky Way a white band above us.

Fifteen.

On November 6, impatient to know what happened to *Virgil*, I called Sam Jacobsen's office. He was there.

I asked if my letter had reached him. He said it had. I asked if he'd found our case number. He said he had not.

He sounded shaken, chagrined. "Do you remember, back in April 1989, when I changed secretaries?"

"Yes," I answered, confused.

"The Petition for Writ of Certiorari got stuck on a shelf and it sat there."

It took a second for this to sink in. "You mean the Supreme Court never *got* it?"

"No," he said. "I assumed these things just take time, I'd crossed it off my mental list, but when the questions started coming in, I discovered it hadn't been sent out of here."

"Oh," I said, adjusting to this, the latest piece of bad news.

"I'm so sorry," he said.

"Sam," I said, trying to lighten the moment, "we all know losing a good secretary can be very costly."

"Yeah," he said.

I told him how grateful we were for all he had done—the time, the trouble, the fine words he'd written. "Does it help," I said jokingly, "if I say I forgive you?"

He said it did.

This left us with two choices, he said. Let it go or send it in with an explanation. "They may take it, they may not. They may say okay, and then the question is, are we happy about it? They may say to hell with it." He was reluctant to go on because the

A.C.L.U. didn't want us to continue, but he'd leave it up to us. "You caucus and let me know what you decide."

We talked about how the Court had moved to the right since 1989. "David Souter and Clarence Thomas aren't doing us much good," he said, "but then if you voted for Reagan or Bush—"

He said his principal reluctance was professional embarrassment about what had happened, but we shouldn't be burdened by this. He was reluctant, though, too, for another reason—the A.C.L.U. didn't want us to continue. "It was a long shot back in 1989 when they dropped the case. It's longer now. Suter and Thomas aren't doing us much good. But then, if you voted for Reagan or Bush—"

I snapped, "Damn it, Sam, that's Susan and Monya!"

His own preference, given the long shot nature of it all, was to let it lie. "The other possibility is to file a motion and they might take it, then the question would be, are we happy about it? It was a long shot before; it's a longer shot now."

I asked if he'd be willing to go before the Supreme Court to argue the case if the motion was granted. He said yes. He'd do whatever we decided.

I called Susan and told her the news. There was a silence before she moaned in her Port. St. Joe drawl, "You mean we have to decide all over again?"

"'Fraid so," I said.

She offered to call Monya in Coeur d'Alene, Idaho.

I called Leanne Katz, director of the National Coalition Against Censorship. She and I had talked off and on during *Virgil*. I told her was Sam had told me. I asked her what she thought we should do.

"Oh, Claudia," she said, "I'm honored you've asked my advice but I have to be honest. I think to go on would be a mistake. It's highly unlikely the Supreme Court would accept the case, but there are so many loose cannons on the Court now, they just might accept it. If they did, I would be terrified. I would want to leave the country. Back in 1989 when you did decide to go on, I was concerned, but it's much more dangerous now."

I mentioned *Hazelwood*, how the courts had misapplied

that decision, how naive they'd been to assume the book wasn't banned.

Leanne disagreed. "*Hazelwood* was not misapplied. The courts aren't naive. *Hazelwood* was a vicious decision and it was viciously applied in your case. The Court now is worse, much worse than we ever thought it would be. Shelving your case may have been a blessing."

"Then you think we should stop."

She sighed. "I know it's hard, but what you have to feel is that part of your enormous commitment is not to go on, that it's more courageous not to continue. It isn't a case of putting your head in the lion's mouth, but the head of the cause."

I agreed.

I called Susan and asked what she and Monya wanted to do.

Susan sighed, too. "I don't much care anymore, and Monya said, 'for her thirty-three percent,' she'll go along with what we decide."

I told her what Leanne Katz had said.

Susan agreed. "Let it end quietly."

An ironic smile crossed my face. "Not with a bang but a whimper."

Later that day I wrote Leanne Katz a letter:

Dear Leanne,

Well, five years and eight months and one day after my husband remarked over cocktails that a minister in Lake City wanted to ban the humanities textbook, we've called it a day. Your advice was important. I couldn't quit until I had the language to tell myself I wasn't a quitter. You gave me that.

I called Sam Jacobson's office, but he wasn't there. I left a message for him to call back.

Sam returned my call two weeks later, November 20, nine-thirty at night. He was still at the office. I was in the kitchen, up to my elbows in pretzels and popcorn filling zip lock bags for

Ross's bake sale at school.

I hooked the receiver under my chin and filled the bags as we talked. I told him we'd decided not to go on; I'd talked to Leanne Katz and she felt it would be too dangerous.

He said he'd had misgivings when we wanted to go on in the first place; he thought it was dangerous then.

"We had misgivings, too," I said. "We were scared of doing more harm than good." I thought of what Leanne Katz had said. "Maybe getting shelved was a blessing."

"Hmm," he mused, "I never thought about that."

"Maybe I have an overly optimistic explanatory style," I explained, "but things may have worked out for the best, given the conservative courts." I assured him there were no ill feelings among us, the three plaintiffs. We admired him and we were grateful for all he had done.

Then I told him about winning in Live Oak. "We may have done some good after all. My husband said the ghost of *Virgil* was there in that room, and I think he was right. I don't think the board remembered that we'd lost in court, but they remembered what a hard time we'd given the board in Lake City."

He said it worked the same way with libel. Years later, people don't remember who won but they remember who said what about whom.

I set a bag of popcorn and pretzels aside. "Sam, do you mean to tell me the real victory is not in the courts, it's in memory?"

He said, "Maybe it is."

Books won't stay banned. They won't burn.
Ideas won't go to jail. In the long run of history,
the censor and the inquisitor have always lost.
The only sure weapon against bad ideas is better ideas.
The source of better ideas is wisdom.
The surest path of wisdom is a liberal education.

—A. Whitney Griswold, American educator
(1906–1963)